Drink While You Can

Lou Vitti

WORD ASSOCIATION PUBLISHERS
www.wordassociation.com
1.800.827.7903

Printed in the United States of America.

ISBN: 978-1-63385-118-4

Library of Congress Control Number: 2015920306

Designed and published by

Word Association Publishers
205 Fifth Avenue
Tarentum, Pennsylvania 15084

www.wordassociation.com

1.800.827.7903

Daniel Okrent wrote a book, *Last Call the Rise and Fall of Prohibition*, a great read and quite the education. If I remember correctly, one of the educational channels, PBS with Ken Burns or History, made a documentary program of it. One of the memorable facts contained in the book is that it was easier to get a drink during Prohibition than it was after Prohibition was repealed.

Pennsylvania is one of the last, if not the last state, to run an exclusive chain of state-controlled liquor stores controlling the importation, sale and consumption of alcoholic beverages in all its many forms. If you think seriously, people go to the corner bar or the fanciest restaurant and the main reason is to get some social activity and amiability with others, oftentimes strangers, while destroying their brain cells, liver and kidneys as well as other parts and removing good sense and clarity of conversation from their presence of mind by drinking. There are many facets regarding the liquor industry including obtaining a license, maintaining a license, opening a place, and have it run according to the rules of the Pennsylvania Liquor Control Board. Every so often a Republican gets to be elected governor of Pennsylvania and attempts to placate the lace curtain supporters by making the liquor industry go into private hands. The complaints are plentiful, mainly lack of variety, usually wine products and the expense that it attached to the single largest monopoly in the Commonwealth, if not the United States.

There are many and varied financial incentives to have the Liquor Control remain as it is in its present form like union employees, revenue to the Commonwealth, business for attorneys, accountants and others. Every time a liquor license is required by your local friend, or a chain hotel, or casino, an application must be submitted and reviewed by an employee of the board in licensing. Then an inspector is assigned to investigate and the application is either denied, approved, or sent back for more information. The quicker the application is approved, the sooner the money flows. The more whiskey that flows is supposed to increase the monetary flow.

After Prohibition, those folks that dealt in liquor, which was prohibited, had to seek other means of income. One way to make money was a gambling system named "Policy." Policy in Harlem was a great venture where a number bet on the last three digits of the stock market or local race track receipts and would pay odds of varying amounts depending whether it was a "cut" number, and so on, but the recovery was always less than the real odds of winning. This was a nice source of income, but after Al Capone went to jail for income tax evasion, the numbers books needed an income to declare. What else? Open a bar.

The problem was, in Pennsylvania, if you had a criminal record you could not own a bar, nor be a shareholder or manager of a drinking establishment. If you had a wife or girlfriend or relative, your problem was partially solved except that you had to explain where the investment money originated for lease, equipment, etc.

As a result of these restriction, various lending companies were then incorporated. These did lending almost exclusively as tavern lenders and for security, the liquor license was secured by a judgment levied against the license for protection. Now came the equipment and supplies. Some of the former bootleggers got into equipment, some into supplies.

Whiskey sours, pina colada, golden Cadillac, whatever, require ingredients to make the drink. Starting a company that supplied all the fruit drinks as a shell company became so lucrative that the three partners quit the policy game (called numbers in Pennsylvania) and went straight, turning it into a multimillion dollar company that they sold years later.

Cigarettes on the premises? Vending machine business. Need added income? Games of chance. Split on the income and even get loans when times were slow to insure the location. Poker machines became a major item in most privately owned bars as they provided a great source of income at not much overhead. The fact that they were illegal did present a problem. If you didn't know the player, you wouldn't pay off, but that ruse only worked for so long. The device that was used to knock off the games was determined by the proceedings before the Hearing Officers at the Liquor Control Board to be a device to enhance a game of chance so that avenue went by the wayside when the Pennsylvania Appeals courts agreed with that position. All these items came about coincidentally as the American thirst for adventure and liquid refreshment continued to spiral upwards after the repeal of Prohibition. There were also those who saw other avenues. The after hours clubs stayed open until the wee small hours. It was necessary that the organization be a valid fraternal club such as Alvito, Sergeant Basilone Club and The IBBA. These became a fashionable exercise and, with card games or barbut games, made an even better impression. With legalized gambling now moving into a legally sanctioned source of income, the government has made the rackets legal and can now tax them and make revenue from a once forbidden fruit. The government also became much more possessive of its newfound source of income and the small fines and slap on the hands meaning no jail time were no longer the usual course. Caught competing with the government was unwise. In conjunction with the efforts of the loss of business, bootlegging now had to go to union organizing of Longshoremen who used to unload the boats, and the drivers who transported the wares now became Teamsters, and the retail liquor business had waitresses and bartenders that needed to be protected. Especially if they were to be able to continue to be able to wear the same clothes and live in the same apartments as they did before, when the bookmakers and bootleggers took them to fancy places on the wife's night to stay at home.

The Hotel, Restaurant Employees and Bartender's Union neatly fit the bill. Organizing could be a problem as in most places, the employees were in the habit of working and moving on. Possibly working their way through college, or hired on a part-time basis only. There were some positive efforts, however, where the hotels had individuals that needed the money as it was their main source of income. Some of the larger establishments, for various reasons, did not have any union problems. If the hotel didn't come to terms, a strike could win public sympathy with other unions and if no deliveries were made or the Laundry Workers Union was not providing clean sheets, it could be a real problem. A problem that, in fact, occurred in many instances. Overall, the union served its members well. It also helped that if a fellow union exec from a different union needed a job for his child or mistress that they could be counted on to come through.

Because of the areas in which I practiced law, I represented a relative of the President of the Restaurant union on a numbers rap. I didn't gouge him on the fee and we had favorable results as this was before the government got into the business as a competitor. We then became friendly and I also became friendly with his friends.

I did liquor license work as well. Noted as one of the three best in the county along with Randy Kottman and a young man, Tom Bailey. Randy and I gave seminars along with a Federal Appeals Judge as to the Liquor Law practice. Why a Federal Appeals Judge, I never knew. Amazing what a great part alcohol has played in American history. Western Pennsylvania was the site of the Whiskey Rebellion that caused President George Washington to send over 12,000 militia troops to disband and rout those demonstrating against the excise tax on their beloved spirits. If they only knew what was to come in the future. I also now wish I had known what was about to happen in my instance.

CHAPTER ONE

"Are Counsel ready to address the jury?"

"Yes, your Honor," I stood and proceeded to greet the jury, advise them that this was the only time an attorney is allowed to speak to the jury and explain the formality of what is happening. Besides the opening address, I went through the usual explanations of how the jury system worked. I then laid out the facts of how the nurse anesthetist had been abandoned by the anesthesiologist and had to try to handle the tachycardia on her own while the doctor was circulating to other theaters of surgery to look on other anesthetized patients. She used the proper medication to slow down the heart rate in the absence of the doctor but over-medicated the patient causing the heart to stop. Efforts to revive were ineffective. I recounted all this and addressed the jury for approximately an hour and a half. After I concluded the damages portion, the judge instructed the jury not to discuss nor make any conclusions at this point, as there was another argument to be had after lunch.

The jury was ushered from the courtroom and the judge told us to be back at 1:30 or even a little earlier if we had anything to discuss. Opposing counsel and I exchanged pleasantries and started to leave.

"Lou."

"Yes, Herb?"

"You still have the claim for excess damages failure to settle within policy limits, don't you?"

"I do."

"Do you really think there is a chance that the jury might give an excess verdict?"

"I'll be up front with you, Herb, I think I have about four of the jury solid in my corner and the amount could possibly come in over the limits. About 8-5 odds your way."

"Would you and your client be willing to accept the policy limits?"

"Are you making that offer?"

Herb glanced at the carrier who nodded yes.

"You saw the answer, Lou."

"I'll ask her over lunch. I'll get back here at 1:15 so that we can advise the court as to any changes."

We left for the Carlton where table ten was waiting for us. Kevin, the owner, knew that we were in a trial and had his staff ready to get us in and out, which was not unusual, but he was always on top of what was needed in a pinch and wanted no screw ups.

My client was a striking redhead. She and her husband had been high school sweethearts, married at the end of college, pursued careers, raised three children to adulthood and a daughter still in college in her final year. She had sold the house and moved to upstate New York. The remaining daughter was enrolled at Saint Vincent's College, a short distance form Pittsburgh and where the Steelers hold their training camps. She and her next oldest brother were present during the entire trial. The eldest brother was living and working in California.

Enzo was working our table that day and arrived with my Manhattan as soon as we sat down. He had a bottle of white and a bottle of red on the tray as well.

"Mr. DiAngelo, she changed on me from red to white last time, so, not being sure, I brought both."

"I'll have the red, thank you."

"And for the young lady?"

Her mother interrupted, "The almost too young lady."

"Ma, I have wine all the time."

"I'll vouch for her age, Enzo, if her mother will allow."

"I'll take the white if Mother is taking the red, thank you. It's a Sauvignon Blanc, I hope, and not a Chardonnay or Pinot."

"Salud to the young lady! Miss, it is a Sauvignon Blanc. We aren't allowed to serve Pinot at Mr. DiAngelo's table."

I acknowledged some friends as they arrived, we ordered our lunch and I brought the proposal of defense counsel to my client's attention.

"The policy limits are $1,500,000.00 plus record costs. If the jury comes in over that amount we will have to make a claim for the excess against the Defendant who will have to make the claim against the carrier. Remember, we haven't heard his closing argument which could be effective and if we get a high award or an excess verdict, the chances are that they will appeal to an appeals court."

"That will mean additional delay over this issue, isn't that correct?"

"I'm afraid so. There is also a chance that the jury could find in the Defendant's favor. Herb did a good job on his case. I don't think he will get the jury verdict but you never know."

"How soon would we get the money?"

"Within six weeks."

"You know that will be the real reason that I will settle. The amounts can never make up for what happened, but it is some compensation and a great amount will go the children in Trust for their futures."

"Are we in agreement that we will settle?"

"Yes."

"Good, let's have another drink, or would you prefer champagne to celebrate?"

Just then Judge Bartolomeo came over.

"Excuse me, Lou, may I interrupt?"

"Sure, your Honor. We're just wrapping up."

"Oh, I'm sorry, I heard that you were trying a medical malpractice case at Judge Smith's. Are these the clients?"

"They are."

"Please accept my apologies for interrupting and, also, I think condolences may also be in order if I'm not mistaken, this was a fatality case."

"Thank you, Judge, it is a fatality case. It was my husband, and you needn't apologize for interrupting. We get interrupted frequently when we are with Mr. DiAngelo."

"I'll bet. Once again, excuse me, but Lou, could you act as a Master for me on a Partition Case?"

"Sure. As long as I have no client conflicts, I'd be happy to do it."

"I'll have a copy of the cover sheet sent over to you for you to see if there is any conflict or other problem. Good luck to all of you on your case."

"We're going back to settle. I completed my closing and Herb Calhoun has yet to close but we are getting the limits to make it an end to an unhappy experience."

"Now you're thinking like a lawyer instead of the shyster that I know you can be."

"Hey! Watch that kind of talk!"

"Thank you. Now, if you'll all excuse me, some of us have to work for a living."

"He seems like a nice enough person."

"He is. Brilliant scholar. Writes some great opinions on civil litigation cases."

We finished our lunch and then we returned to the courtroom. I advised Herb, we advised the Judge. The judge then had the jury reconvene where he thanked them and advised that they had performed their duty and because of their efforts the case wasn't going any further.

We all exchanged amenities and I headed back to the office to see what was next on my calendar.

"What's up guys?"

"Leo called, something about his New York property. Rosa Simeone called regarding her nephew being in some trouble. The bartender from Bob's garage called, said it was personal, and somebody named Sam called. Said he was Tony's friend. Needed some liquor help. Same message from a guy who said to tell you the Greek called. You should spend more time around the office."

"I was out earning everybody's salary for this year. I'll take the messages, thanks."

I got Rosa on the first try.

"Louie, how are you?"

"Couldn't be better, Rosa, how are you?"

"I'm fine but these kids are going to put me in an early grave. You know Tom Eveready, the attorney?"

"Yeah, I know him."

"He is representing some young kid that my son-in-law was fighting. Said he might have to file criminal charges if we can't work it out."

"What does he want to work out?"

"You remember Skippy, the one who married Maria. You were at the wedding at the Center City Hotel."

"I really don't, but why the big fuss?"

"Well, the kids go up to the ball field every day and they play pick up games. Apparently, Skippy and this other boy got into an argument over who was out and about being tagged in the head and one thing lead to another, they got into a fight and now Skippy got a call from Eveready, the attorney."

"You know Tom, don't you, Ro?"

"Sure, but I didn't want to call in case I might say something wrong. I figured I'd have you call."

(I thought to myself, what did I ever do to deserve such generosity? I get to make the call. Oh, well, she does favors for everybody and has done them for me, as well. I got an appointed spot with the courts because of Rosa for a couple years as a zoning referee until the administration changed.)

"Did Tom say anything about what he wanted?"

"I don't think so."

"I'll give Tom a call. A scuffle in a schoolyard- how bad can it be? I'll get back to you as soon as I find out anything."

Tom had defended some big criminal cases a few years back. They were mostly non-violent, high profile bookmakers and numbers cases and Tom was a studious lawyer playing on the nuances of the law. There was a requirement to get a tax stamp which he successfully argued was a violation of Fifth Amendment right against self-incrimination when you were running a book joint and it became one of the classic arguments.

I decided to return the call from the Greek before calling Eveready.

"Hello."

"Steve, Lou DiAngelo."

"Hello, Counselor. Can we meet somewhere? Maybe the Howard Johnson's in Monroeville or King's Restaurant out that way?"

"Why, what's up?"

"Some people from out New Ken way may need some help. Sam was trying to get some stuff done for his guy regarding a liquor license. One of his relatives wanted a $5,000 ticket to get him a Sunday Sales license. I need to talk to you about it."

"I already got a call from Sam."

"Already? Good. I need to see you about some other things, as well. Come on, Counselor, you have to meet me. Didn't I come to your side when you needed me?"

"I'll see you on my way home, about 3:30 or 4:00. I want to beat most of the heavy traffic. I'll see you at Howard Johnson's at the bar."

"Thank you, I really need you, Counselor."

Some years back, my lady was stopping in a local bar for lunch on occasion, meeting with her other lady friends when this wise guy, a local car salesman, started hitting on her every week. He apparently figured out their luncheon routine. In spite of the fact that she kept telling him to beat it, he wouldn't stop. I asked the Greek if he knew him, as the Greek used to dabble in the car business. He did know him and without any further questions took it upon himself to pay a visit to the lot. The salesman left town for a month. I never knew what happened but the bartender in the luncheon place asked me if it was all right for him to come back. I said yes after I instructed the Greek to not do anything and inquired what he had done. He explained that he merely had a conversation. I'll bet.

Next call.

"Leo Parks, please. Thank you."

"Uncle Leo here."

"Lou DiAngelo, you called."

"Hey, Louie, thanks. How you doing?"

"Couldn't be better. What's up?"

"I got a subpoena from the U.S. Attorney in upstate New York. Wants to talk to me about that property you got your friend to sell for me a while back."

"What does the subpoena say?"

"Not much. Just for me to appear and bring all rental records and all other records regarding the building."

"As I remember, when my friend Bruce sent the process server to the property, the people in the house fired some shots at him."

"That's right but why do they want me?"

"Information. It's probably a fact gathering inquest. Can you fax the subpoena to me? I'll look into it for you. Not sure what you can tell them. In the meantime, get all your information together with regard to the rental amounts, payments and people."

"Thank you. God bless you. I'm glad you're my friend."

"I didn't do anything yet."

"Hello, Bob's Garage."

"Alana there? This is Lou DiAngelo."

"This is she. Oh, thanks for calling me back. Can I make an appointment to see you? You do divorces, don't you?"

"Yes, ma'am."

"Good, can I get in to see you this week?"

"How about Thursday? What's your work schedule?"

"I usually work lunch Thursday but I'll get Barb to switch with me. What time?"

"How about 11:00?"

"Perfect. Where are you located?"

"Down near Market Square on 4th Avenue."

"You used to be near the arena, weren't you?"

"Yes, I was, but with the renewal up there, I sold that building. Now I'm a downtown guy, no longer an uptown guy."

"See you on Thursday."

I hung up and made the call that was going to be the most important one of the day, I was sure.

"Hello."

"Sam, Lou DiAngelo."

"Luigi! How you doing? Hold it, sorry I asked, 'Best I ever was', I know."

"Close enough."

"Listen, Luig, my guy needs some help. You still do liquor stuff, right?"

"I do."

"What do you need to get us a Sunday sales license for the club?"

"Well, I'll need to have your accountant get me all the records of sales and sign an affidavit of the percentage of sales from whiskey and food and all that type information."

"No, no, no. I mean what do YOU need, like money?"

"Probably $550 to $1,000."

"Not any more?"

"No, why?"

"My guy has a nephew who is an attorney. He wanted five large. I ain't trying to make you a cheap whore, we know all lawyers have a rep as being whores and I don't want to make it look like I'm cheapening you, but I'm kinda shocked you're so low."

"The kid may not be sure of what he had to do, and, may have been hedging his bets or else he is a pig, just like all you wise guys."

"Hey, hey, hey. Okay, okay, I had that one coming. You got me. When can I see you?"

"You want to come to town?"

"Not unless I was under arrest. Can I meet with you at Franco's in Harmarville? That's out your way, no?"

"When did you have in mind?"

"The sooner the better."

"I just finished up a jury trial. I'm a little whipped and I have a lot of things backed up. Maybe tomorrow after work or the next day."

"Let me give you a number to call. Leave a message and they will get it to me and we can meet whenever you say. Thank you. You will make my guy very happy."

"Also, Sam, it makes you look good saving him money as well but not looking so good for his nephew."

"It's his brother's wife's sister's kid. No harm. He don't like that family anyhow."

"I'll be in touch."

Sam was responsible for the day to day. He was the most trusted of all the people with this guy. The money was always the right count and they were closer than brothers.

Finally, the end. All caught up at this point. Have the mail to get through and then on to the Inn to meet with the Greek.

"Who knows what evil lurks in the hearts of men?"

Forget the Shadow. Nobody does.

CHAPTER TWO

The parking lot was filled, as usual, with a great many cars. The lot was used for parking by people getting on the PA Turnpike with a friend or for getting a bus to another destination. The owner didn't complain. He maintained a great relationship with everybody in the area and did a very good bar trade, also receptions for weddings, political fundraisers, and other such events.

There were two bars in the building but the closest to the entrance and the darkest one was where most of my clients waited to have meetings.

The Greek was at the far end. Appeared to be drinking a fruit drink.

"Lou, thanks for coming. Do you want to sit so we can talk?"

"Whatever you say. I can talk at the bar or at a table."

There was nobody at the bar, but his sense of caution made him decide to move to this table.

"I need you to do something for me. I need to be able to carry again. I have some opportunities coming up and I need to be able to complete what I am asked to do."

"What is it that you have in mind for me to do and for you to be able to do?"

"One of the old guys wants me to provide some insurance protection for him. It's a big chance for me to get in good and look forward to not having to just do what I have been doing for too long."

"How is it that I can help?"

"I need you to clean up my record."

"You want an expungement?"

"Yeah, that's it, what you said, where I have no record anymore."

"That's a little difficult. You have a conviction. First you have to get a pardon from the Governor. You understand we have to file a Petition requesting the Pardon, have a hearing before a review board and then the Governor has to sign. After that we have to file a Petition for Expungement of your record. After we get an order of court granting expungement, then we have to convince the Bureau of Criminal Identification to destroy the records. The State Police sometimes have their counsel object and then possibly a third hearing. One of the line items needed on the application is your occupation. What are you doing for that?"

"I have a job that I can list as a car lot supervisor. I can get that confirmed."

"I hear what you're saying but it's not a quick process."

"You'll do it as fast as you can, I know. How much will it cost?"

"How much do you have?"

"I'll get whatever you need."

"Figure $3-5,000, depending. You know I'll try to give you the best I can but it is a lot of work."

"I understand. Now, I have something for you."

"What?"

"The liquor license you got. Well, that's straight from the old man. He's not happy with what has been going on with the attorney they use now."

"You mean his nephew?"

"No, not him. That was just a favor he was trying to do. The other guy, the Jew attorney."

"Sam Blueman?"

"Yeah, that's him. He did something that got the old guy upset. I didn't hear what but he was hot. There was a coffee meeting at the other place down the road. I happened to be there. So, what I am telling you, Counselor, be careful. The old guy already has had it with attorneys and you also know, crime never wants to pay."

"Thanks. I'll send you some papers to sign and return to me with a check and I'll get started."

"Thanks, I knew I could count on you."

"Don't get too excited, I'm just starting to see what I can do. I may not be able to get it done."

I called Annie on the way to my car for her to send a Power of Attorney and forms to the Greek. We had his address in the

Plum area on an old file and for some odd reason, I knew it from memory.

The day was drawing to a close and getting dark. I didn't see the two men at first who were in the alcove outside the main entrance. They were walking in my direction and at a quick pace so I turned and faced them and nodded, "Hello, Gentlemen." They slowed down. No wing tips. No white shirts.

"You Lou DiAngelo?"

"Who wants to know?"

"That's him. Can you take a few minutes to take a ride with us?"

"What about, guys? I've had a long day."

"Give us about 15 minutes."

"How about right here?"

They looked around and the shorter stockier one seemed satisfied. "How about you take us around behind the main building in your car? May be best no one sees us together."

"Sounds like a plan, jump in."

We pulled around to the back of the Inn.

"What can I do for you?"

"You got a call from Sam the other day, right?"

"Hold on. Before I go any further, maybe we ought to all know who we are. You seem to know who I am and probably that I'm a lawyer. Who and what are you?"

"Fair enough. I'm JoJo. This is Chuckie Z. We work for the old guy. He has some beefs that he was interested in finding out. You was just with the Greek. What was that about?"

"Sorry, guys, I can't talk about a client's business with anyone. Just like I couldn't talk what and if I am doing anything for the person that you say is your boss. And, if I could, how would I know that you really were who you said you were. For all I know, you could be FBI."

The short, stocky one nodded and looked like he wanted to laugh. He smiled.

"Pretty good, pretty good. I guess that's fair enough. How about I ask you some questions and see if you can help me do what I get paid to do. You was just with the Greek, right?"

"That's right."

"He wasn't asking you about any liquor license stuff, was he?"

"No."

"Did he ask you to get involved in a liquor license transfer in this area and not out near New Ken?"

"No."

"Now, I'm taking you at your word."

"Gentlemen, I don't lie and, in spite of that, you give me no reason to lie."

"Ok. Thank you, Counselor. We can walk from here. Have a good night. If we need to see you again can we give you a call?"

"It's 'May I give you a call'. Sure. Here's a card. Call any time."

"Thank you."

I pulled out and headed for home. Maybe I might stop on the way home and grab dinner. It was still a nice day and I could use a little break. I was on the Turnpike heading home and had several choices. Cala Lily was close to home but I had just been there a couple of nights before, so Franco's was the easy call.

The parking lot had a good number of cars. For a week night, it looked like a fair crowd.

Maureen was surprised pleasantly, I hope, to see me. I hadn't called ahead.

"Hello, darling. Alone tonight?"

"Yeah, I just finished a week's worth of work and figured I better have something good to eat. Couldn't think of any place nearby that was good, so I came here."

"Hey, watch that. We might think you're serious."

"Why do you think I keep coming back? Until you get it right."

"Ok with Pete waiting on you? Maureen the Waitress is off tonight."

"That's nice, one on, one off, one manager at a time. Sure, Pete's OK. He can only serve what the cook puts on the tray."

"I have a table in his section that should be no problem. Will you be having a glass or a bottle of wine?"

"A glass of Macallan and a bottle of wine. Maybe a DaVinci Chianti. Whatever I don't finish can be for your enjoyment later."

"That's a deal. How hungry are you?"

"Hungry enough, but I'll skip the appetizers and just have a house salad and the salmon and bow ties with the tomato cream sauce."

"I'll tell Pete. Meantime, Frank will send you something anyhow. Either greens and beans or ricotta meatballs. He was putting some things together before you got here so you lucked out."

"Thanks."

Lori walked over from the bar with the Macallan.

"I heard you say you needed a drink. Did I guess right?"

"On the button, thank you."

It felt good to unwind. I looked up and saw the front door open and Sam, Tony and the Greek walked in. I wanted to duck out the back door or slide under the table, but it looked like the damned night was not about to end. They looked up, saw me, waved and here they came.

"Counselor, how about that, first guess was right. I said he'd be here."

"Gentlemen, how nice of you to drop by. Does this mean I'm buying dinner or were you picking up my check?"

"Nobody is that strong, Counselor. I remember I wanted to buy him a drink, he had just walked in and the check was a buck and a half. He had one of those whatever he drinks and bought everybody at the bar a drink on his first move in the place. Lucky for me I forgot my wallet. Anyhow, how you doing?"

"Since I last spoke to you, couldn't be better."

"Let's have a couple of minutes before your dinner comes, please?"

"You asked nice, Sam, what's up?"

"I see where some guys wanted to talk to you after you were done with the Greek here."

"So?"

"I also know that they were sent and that you didn't tell them anything. Remember no one can ever be too sure. The old guy is always asking what else can be done, and, in this instance, backup questioners got you a passing mark."

"And that means you're still not picking up my dinner check?"

Tony hadn't said a word. That was his style. He smiled and laughed a lot but never got himself in trouble by saying anything that could get in a bind. The Greek was also tight-lipped, maybe because it looked like he was part of the setup earlier.

"We just wanted you to know that we always knew we could count on you, but old habits never die. Old guys might, but not old suspects. Well, if you'll forgive us. Hear from you soon."

Sam and Tony got up and started for the door.

The Greek paused and leaned over.

"You know I had no part in that deal, right? Never mind. Open this in the bathroom later."

He slipped me a small container, like a band-aid tin and left with the other two.

The greens and beans arrived in a red-based sauce. Not like the Calabrese style, which is usually in a white stew type sauce. It was delicious as were the ricotta meatballs.

The wine arrived and Pete was doing his best. He had to say hello to the three of them as they left since his family had a long history with this crew.

I went to wash my hands in the men's room before the main course arrived. I opened the tin. A bullet and a match were in the tin. The Greek was telling me that he would make sure anything that I needed to be done, by gun or flame, would be his favor to me. I wondered if he meant anything with regard to the other two. I was certain that this was not another loyalty test. The Greek has a funny way of showing his appreciation, but appreciative he was. We had an experience years before when a couple of wanna-be wise guys intruded on our table in a small restaurant. He had an explosive temper and, before I knew it, both of the kids were on the floor and bleeding. He was that quick and that deadly. His younger brother and I were friendlier. Maybe it was the age difference. The brother was just as quick if not quicker, and just as deadly.

My cell phone rang. It was Lola.

"It used to be that I would get to have a meal once in a while. Is there something that you want to tell me or is there something that I don't want to hear?"

"I stopped to grab a quick bite at Franco's in Harmarville on my way home from a very, very long and eventful day. I almost went directly home from my last meeting but decided to indulge myself and even that didn't work out too well."

"Dining alone. That must be true because you would never expect anybody to believe that."

"Don't worry. My case is over. Maybe lunch tomorrow or dinner or both?"

"Am I being too pushy?"

"You mean are you acting like a possessive pain in the ass bitch, or were you referring to something else?"

"Don't sugarcoat it, tell me what you really feel."

"I feel like I am loved by the most wonderful woman in the world who will only want the best for me and will do everything she can to make my life great."

"WOW!!"

"Now, all I have to do is find that woman."

"I hope your hickey falls off."

"I'm sure that you don't, but we can both go look for it tomorrow. Now, if you don't mind, I am going to finish the meal and end up in my nice bed for a good night's sleep."

"I love you."

"Likewise, I'm sure."

"Likewise, I'm sure, that's the best you can do? Why am I asking? See you tomorrow."

The thought crossed my mind. Would they really send two guys to check on me? This wasn't like trying to get someone to roll over and chirp. Maybe trying to impress me with a cautionary note. How else could they have been so close by? Wouldn't be worth it to have a tail on me. All that for another day. I pulled into the garage and went to the downstairs bar, lit a short Cuban and poured a Chartreuse. The drink at over 100 proof is better than sleeping pills, those Carthusian Monks that make it must sleep like logs.

Caught a little bit of the news on TV and saw where there had been a sweep of drug dealers and stolen cars in upstate New York. The cars were being sent overseas to the Middle East. The usual fires and shootings by suspected gang members, the weather would be pleasant and the daily number. It wasn't a number I would have played so I saved my money again.

Another slug of Chartreuse and sleep was to be sound and uneventful as no pressing cases to keep me awake or cause me to wake at 3:00 A.M. with anxiety attacks.

CHAPTER THREE

"Hello, this is Attorney Lou DiAngelo for Attorney Eveready. Thank you, yes, I can hold."

His secretary was checking to see if he was available to talk.

"Good morning, Lou, how are you?"

"Couldn't be better, Tom, how's everything with you?"

"Great. To what do I owe the pleasure of this call?"

"You represent one of two young men involved in a fight at the city playground the other day. I was asked to represent the other guy. The mother-in-law is a friend of mine and she wants me to see if I can get this all cleaned up."

"Do you know the young man?"

"I'm told I was at his wedding, but not really. My lady client tells me he's a good kid, just on disability and trying to get up and around."

"You're the best. You always have the saints and the other guy always has the sinners."

"How's that?"

"You haven't seen the police report yet, have you?"

"No, why?"

"Let me save you a little trouble. I'll fax it over to you, but let me tell you what your recovering disabled man did to my sinner. He didn't use the bat to hit any balls out of the park but he tried to hit my guy for a homerun. He then tried to keep the other people who were there from helping break up the brawl with the same bat. I have all the statements from the other people that were there, as well as the neighbors who live near the park. From what I found out, your guy has a mean temper and a mean streak that could make Jack the Ripper look tame. Now, I know you do the same kind of work that I do, Lou, but you should know that my guy has a broken arm and suffered a mild concussion. It would have been worse if your guy hadn't hit my fella's arm when he was aiming for his head. Your guy might then be facing a murder one charge. Now the police have scheduled a preliminary hearing tentatively for ten days from yesterday. They are trying to serve the warrant on your guy. What do you think we can do to work this out?"

"What does your guy want?"

"He's really not too greedy. Then again, what does he gain from your guy being guilty? And if he wants to try to sue, what kind of recovery will he get from your guy? Finally, your guy isn't in trouble for the first time. He strong armed some guys that were trying to buck the Bartender's Union organization at a local restaurant chain a couple of years ago. Make your day seem a little better already?"

"Holy shit, all that so soon. You look like you did your homework."

"Not hard when the police provided it all over the computer from BCI and a little conversation. Listen, you and I have worked together before. See what you can do. This time I really do have the saint and you've really got the sinner."

"Thanks, Tom, let me see what I can do. Any idea of a number?"

"Since there is no liability insurance and since his medicals have been paid, it will be a reasonable number. You will have to get Blue Cross to waive their subrogation and I'll talk to the kid about $10,000.00. He may be ok with something in that area, and I get to have my time reimbursed."

"I'll see how this flies. I'll get back to you."

"Mr. D?"

"Yes, Annie."

"I've got Bruce Bergman from New York on the phone."

"Thanks. Hey, Bruce, how you doing?"

"Don't give me that shit."

"Whoa, what caused that?"

"That property I sold for your guy a while back, well, the U.S. Attorney and the DEA and ATF are all calling me. I spoke with the U.S. Attorney and he told me that the place was running women and that a meth lab had been set up there."

"What's that have to do with you? My guy has been served with a subpoena and that is one of my calls for this morning. All you did was an Action is Ejectment and threw out whoever was in the place doing whatever they were doing."

"Yeah, but who needs federal headaches."

"Tell you what, give me the name of the U.S. Attorney and his phone number and I'll see what I can do to substitute my guy and me for you. I had to call him anyway."

"No problem, I'll switch you over to my administrative assistant and she'll give you that info. Before I do, though, how are you doing, really?"

"Couldn't be better."

"I had to hear it. Everything is ok, really?"

"Thank God, everything is Jake."

"Ok, now see what you can do to keep me from wasting time with these other guys. Maybe I can send you a similar case sometime."

Now, I had to figure out which way to turn first. Probably the easiest first and save the tough for last.

I called Rosa. She answered her work phone on the third ring.

"Rosa, Lou DiAngelo."

"Sweetheart, how are you?"

"I'm fine but your son-in-law is in a bit of a jackpot."

"How so?"

"It wasn't just a punching match. It seems that he went to work on the other kid with a baseball bat. It's a good thing your son-in-law didn't kill him."

"What are you trying to say, Lou?"

"The other kid is pretty banged up and needed hospital care. Your kid was a little crazy and was trying to take off his head with the bat. The medicals may be covered, and the insurance company may request reimbursement if they find out, and the injured boy wants to try to come to a money result. In short, you can buy your way out if you want to, but only if it's soon before the preliminary hearing next week."

"What's the tariff?"

"The first figure I heard was $10,000 plus something for Tom Eveready. Probably fourteen large ought to do it."

"Where is he supposed to get the money?"

"I don't know. Maybe hold up a bank with a baseball bat. That's your call. I can only tell you what is going on and what you or somebody needs to do to make it go away. Maybe you want to think about it and get back to me?"

"Yes, let me call you tomorrow."

"I'll call Tom and see what can be done to delay."

I then called Eveready and he, fortunately, was available.

"Is this the only case you have, Lou, or are you getting a large hourly?"

"Don't I wish. My client's folks want to see if they can get a little time to get their act together and deal with this. I can't promise anything except that they are going to figure out what to do."

"Well, you're living right. The arresting officer is going on vacation and they asked if they could continue for thirty days. As a matter of routine, I said ok. Does that help?"

"You're an angel, Tom. Thanks."

I called Rosa and told her. She thought that I did something great and now I could put that one off my to do list.

I started on the package from Judge Bartolomeo's chambers where he asked me to act as a Master. It was a family dispute over the property of the mother between two sons and a daughter. The son lived in the one property rent-free for years paying taxes and maintaining the property, leading him to feel he now had a superior right to the land and house on it. There were three other properties as well in the case, all in different sections of town and all owned differently. One in a tract, one in all names and one just in the mother's name. The total value couldn't be more than $400,000.00 considering the locations, but a real estate appraiser would determine that. I called the judge to see when he could hear my petition to have me appointed as I saw no conflict with the parties involved and he gave me a morning later that week. I called my friend and real estate broker, Rich Creo, since I would need his services.

"Counselor, how you doin'?"

"Couldn't be better, Duke, how are you doing?"

"Like you say, couldn't be better, and I use it as well and give you credit."

"I'm going to need you on a case that I have to decide. There is a partition action regarding four properties. Once I decide who gets what, I will need to know the value of the four houses. Two in Munhall, one in Greenfield and one in Morningside. I can scan over the addresses and the info from the county web site to see if you can handle. I'll also need to have an idea of the charges for your service."

"How soon do you need the reports?"

"Not for a while. I haven't even been appointed yet."

"Good. I have a load of items to get through on assessment appeals and I have 3-4 closings coming up. I can probably get to it in about two to three weeks."

"That will be better than good."

"You know what, I was going to call you. You remember my cousin, John Delacroce, Fish's younger brother?"

"Yes, I remember him. I think I represented him in a domestic a lot of years back."

"Well, of all things, his uncle was a cop, his father did time, and now this kid gets arrested for growing marijuana in his back yard. The township police arrested him in Bridgeville."

"That's great. Oh, well, I have a friend on that force. He'll fill me in. Understand that doesn't mean John will go free with a medal and ribbons. On the other hand, if I recall, he has no record and should be eligible for some program that gets him out of the criminal system and into a rehabilitation setup."

"His father and uncle knew of you and will want to meet with you about this case."

"They want to meet with me?"

"That's what they said. They have some guy that works for the judges in the courthouse that is trying to help this along."

"Just what I need. Help from an accommodation specialist."

"Can I have them call you?"

"Sure."

"Oh, let me know when you want me to do something on those properties."

"Get me your probable fees and I will get them approved by the court."

I then called Roger, my friend on the force in Bridgeville.

"Mr. DiAngelo, how are you?"

"Couldn't be better, Rog, and you?"

"Hey, I'm on the right side of the grass and eating regularly. What can I do for you?"

"There was an arrest of a Delacroce kid for growing marijuana. Know anything about it?"

"Are you going to be on the case?"

"Probably."

"What are you doing around lunchtime?"

"Sounds like I'm buying you lunch. Your place or mine?"

"I'll come to you. I have to go to the courthouse for an arraignment today. How about Ruth's Chris? That's near your place, no?"

"Good deal. I'll call Erin and make a reservation for 11:30, ok?"

"Make it later, about 12:30, sometimes the judges run overtime."

"Done."

Roger was as good as his word and he appeared at 12:30. Erin had already seated me and the staff stopped by to say hello. Jim was taking care of the table and Larry, the manager, had my

Manhattan from Marcie, the bartender. Roger waved off the drink offer from Jim and settled for iced tea and water.

"How did you get involved in the case, Counselor?"

"I'm being recruited, why?"

"When we made the arrest we found some other items in the house. Appears they were stolen. We also received contact from the county police and state police that they are looking at this guy as a person of interest in several areas."

"Receiving stolen property, marijuana, that's not too bad."

"I haven't spoken with the state but you may be facing the Attorney General's office as well as the DA on this cookie."

"Is there anything I should know?"

"Nothing else I know, but since you were getting involved, I though you should get a heads up. Besides, I get to have a free lunch at a nice place."

"Hey, Jim, give him the check please."

"Whatever you say, Mr. DiAngelo."

"Now, what else can you tell me, Rog, so I can rescind that order?"

"Not much more. I will tell you what I can and I will ask the other people on the case if I am able to tell you any of the information. It's all discovery material anyhow, but some guys are hard ons."

We finished our lunches and parted ways. The case still didn't look too bad. RSP and possession of marijuana didn't rate any jail time.

Returned across the square to the office and saw a message from Tony or Sam. Both on the return call note. I called the number.

"Hello, this is Attorney Lou DiAngelo returning your call."

"Hey, Counselor, this is Tony. How you doin'?"

"Couldn't be better. What's the call?"

"How are you doing with the license issue?"

"It's in Harrisburg. Should be processed this week and done by next week. All it takes is a review of the information provided by the accountant. He swears to it on the life of his license and the PLCB approves. If they find out he's lying, they call the Bureau of Professional and Occupational Affairs and try to lift his ticket. Is there a problem?"

"No, it's better than that. The old guy wants to know if you can do a transfer of the license to a new owner. He wants to have the license in the name of his kids to protect them. Right now it's in Sam's name. Not that he doesn't trust Sam, but if something happens to Sam it might get sticky. You know Sam and his wife are having a beef so one thing might lead to another and well, I don't have to tell you what can happen, do I?"

"I understand. You realize that this is a little more difficult than the Sunday Sales application."

"How much tougher?"

"About $5,000 tougher."

"Counselor! You're kidding!"

"I don't joke about money or what I do for a living."

"Ok, I'll tell the old man. I'll get back to you."

"Take care."

Back to work on the Partition case. After about an hour, Jennifer buzzed me.

"Lola calling, shall I put her through?"

"Please."

"Hello, Stranger."

"Stranger than what?"

"Than every other guy that I've seen today. Every guy I saw at lunch wanted to buy me a drink. Why can't I even get the chance to buy you a drink?"

"You have to quit going to bars with judges and attorneys."

"Why?"

"You think Lady Justice is blindfolded and in a flimsy no bra outfit for no good reason? Every attorney and judge wants to take advantage of her sexually. That's why defendants in cases always think they got screwed. It's what the legal profession likes to do. Demonstrate power over others, especially women. I'll bet you ate at the Terrace Room at the William Penn Hotel, or am I wrong?"

"You're right, but how did you guess?"

"There are beds nearby. Attorneys are notoriously flagrante delicto."

"Boy, you are on a tear."

"Probably because I need a drink and you are close by, yes, I'll buy you a drink and dinner and anything else you want. Let me call you back in about an hour to set a time and place."

"Does your description about judges and attorneys include women in the profession?"

"There is no gender inequality in the legal profession. At least not with this office. I deal with a lot of good and bad from both sexes. It used to be, however, that female attorneys had to try harder because of the good old boy type network. I was lucky. I got to work with a lot of good ladies. Some of the drawbacks for those not so good are that they are young and not street smart. The other end is that they think they are hot stuff because they work for a big firm. You experience all that at your office, I am sure."

"You're right. What do you think of Hilary Weisman?"

"Great domestic lawyer. I don't know what other areas of the law she practices. Why do you ask?"

"One of the partners was found to be staying late at the office and not working on case problems and now his wife is creating new ones for him."

"Ouch!"

"You can say that again. We received a five pound package of pleadings from Hilary today."

"Well, she has to represent her client. She's reasonable and her husband is also a family law practitioner. He's good as well. His last name is Levy. She keeps her name. Listen, I have to get some things done or we'll never get together. I'll tell you what, it's getting late enough. Why don't you call when you are leaving and I'll meet you at the garage and we'll go to Cioppono's for drinks and dinner with espresso and dessert at my place."

"May I bring a bag with me?"

"As long as it's a small one, I drove the Corvette in today."

"It's small and so is the vette so we can get cozy. I am always prepared."

"Goodbye."

I went back to finalizing the issues that I saw in the initial pleadings and dictated the Motion for Appointment Acceptance and started to wrap up.

"Mr. DiAngelo, a man says to tell you the Greek is on the line."

"Send it through."

"Hello, Counselor."

"Steve, how can I help you?"

"Can you stop out in Monroeville after work?"

"I wasn't going that way. I expect to join with my lady friend for dinner and probably going to Cioppino's to see Chef Greg for a drink and dinner. Can you stop by there?"
"Where is it and what's the name again?"

"Cioppino's and it is off Smallman Street, around the 2400 block. I expect I'll be there in about an hour. That should give you enough time to make it, don't you think?"

"I don't like going into town. Maybe tomorrow."

"What's the problem anyway?"

"It's the old guy. I think somebody has his ear and I need to find out what's going on."

"How about you come to town tomorrow, or, I can meet you for lunch in Bloomfield at Alexander's."

"Hey, that's great. Alex's place in Bloomfield. Perfect. What time?"

"12:30 ok?"

"It's a deal, I'll see you then."

"Mr. DiAngelo, Lola on the line."

"Hello, gorgeous."

"I am about ready to walk down, but it looks a little wet outside. Would it be too much…"

"No trouble at all. I'll pick you up. It better not be raining too hard though, Corvettes aren't supposed to be out in the rain."

"I'll be down front with my overnighter."

"What will the neighbors on Fourth Avenue think, my, my."

"I hope they suspect that what will happen is what I'm looking forward to getting."

"Drinks and dinner? How did they guess?"

I wrapped up the office and to the garage and up to her building. She was out front with a garment bag and one of those suitcase sized purses that can carry a horse. I managed to squeeze her stuff in the back of the Corvette.

"Hello, Handsome," and a kiss on the cheek. She grabbed my hand and slipped it on her thigh. "Hope we are having oysters tonight, I'd like to be sure that you can and will want to perform."

"Is that all you think about?"

"Sometimes, and this is one of those times."

"It will wait until after dinner, I'm sure."

"Hey, I feel something coming to life."

"Please, I have to shift gears and I don't want to grab the wrong stick or gearbox so behave until it's time to misbehave."

With not too much trouble, we got through the few blocks and the valet was thrilled to park the vette. We went to the bar, which was busy enough for early in the evening. Nicole poured a Macallan for me and presented the wine list.

My cell phone rang and I answered.

"Luigi, Sam. I am here with Tony and we were wondering if we might buy you a drink?"

"Offering to buy in the first sentence means you must be desperate. You guys never buy. Unfortunately, although I would like to take advantage of you, I'm already spoken for."

"Come on, Counselor, you know we can do better."

"I've seen both of your mugs before and I can assure you what's beside me is much better. Take a rain check for tomorrow or another day that suits you but I'm off the clock for today."

"You sure we couldn't bring over a sweetener to change your mind?"

"Let me see if I can make this clear. I'm hanging up the phone and turning it off. Call me tomorrow or some other day. Goodbye."

"That was sure a definite. One of your favorite people?"

"A pushy client who wanted to trade some time for a beautiful young thing that would do my bidding."

"Did you tell them you already had one?"

"They said young thing, not just thing."

"You bastard."

"Are you drinking red or white?"

"Red."

"End of that argument, wasn't it?"

"How young would she have been?"

"Probably too young to drink."

"How much fun could that have been?"

"Well, it would have been cheaper."

"How much do I cost you? I'm a cheap date."

"You win. I'm sorry, just a little tired. What do you say we eat and be friendly."

"Just what I had in mind, or didn't you hear me before?"

Greg was off for the night but the staff in the kitchen didn't miss a step. The food was excellent and the service kept us moving to the end. We skipped the cigar room for the night as I was truly tired. We headed for home and the clouds were getting ugly. I saw a car pull out from the curb after us but paid it not too much mind. It pulled up at the red light beside us and the window came down. It was the Greek.

"Lou, are you able to stop?"

"Steve, I have company, do you see?" And I pointed to Lola.

"Oh, Counselor, I'm sorry. I wasn't sure you wouldn't be too busy tomorrow so I took a chance."

"See you tomorrow, Steve."

The rest of the ride was uneventful.

"He must really need to meet with you."

"Everybody needs help and everybody wants it yesterday. It just can't happen fast enough."

We pulled into the garage and she nibbled at my ear then began cleaning it with her tongue. Amazing how those things work better than Q-tips. She then took my face and launched a kiss that would have caused the invasion of Normandy. Forget Helen of Troy.

We made it to the downstairs TV room and she was in third gear. What man isn't helpless when the woman he loves wants to prove her love and ability to please? The couch was welcoming and roomy enough for all the acrobatics God intended for simians of higher and lower orders.

I was reminded of "Five Easy Pieces" with Jack Nicholson and Sally Struthers as we roamed the room while circling and locked in heavenly embrace falling back on the sofa and rolling with each movement bringing greater pleasure. She moaned and groaned with delight as I tried to maintain my various positions and then all went bright as we ended the journey to Nirvana. It was not easy to disengage as we neither had anything handy like a wipe and were only half naked. I shuffled over to the bath with my pants around my ankles and provided towels. We then embraced again.

"It's been too long, Lou, I miss you."

"I miss you, too, but neither of us forgot anything as soon as we got inside. The house I mean."

"Thanks for having me over."

"I get great pleasure and you thank me. What a deal. Would you care for espresso or coffee?"

"I don't want you to go to any trouble."

"Ok, espresso and ice cream. You can wait here if you like and I will bring it down."

"This couch is so comfortable I could stay here all night. And every night."

"I'll bring the espresso to bring you back to your senses."

The espresso was great and the ice cream is always welcome. She looked at me and we started kissing. Before long, we were once again on the way to meeting all the wishes we had as kids and doing all the things that you do when you don't have to rush. Each touch was on the money and we went for round two. After that, only sleep could be dessert.

CHAPTER FOUR

We were both up and moving before dawn. Both in different showers, I had been downstairs as we did make it to sleep in the bedroom upstairs. I started the coffee and put bacon in the microwave.

"Breakfast will be ready in a few minutes."

"I need to finish dressing. I may need you to help button this dress."

"How do you do it when I'm not around?"

"I get the paper delivery boy to come in."

"That's funny. It's probably Jimmy McGregor and I doubt he would leave easily."

"It's just easier and I like having you dress and undress me."

"Tell me when you need me. I'm going to finish getting ready. I already ate. You are the one who decides when we leave now."

A little bit of final clean up and we were on our way.

My cell phone rang. It was Francie.

"What's up?"

"There are a couple of detectives here wanting to see you. I told them to have a seat. How long before you're here?"

"About twenty minutes. Any reason why they are there?"

"Not that they told me or that I could gather but they seemed ok."
"I'll be there in a little bit."

No wrecks, traffic was normal, I was there in about 20-25 minutes.

I dropped Lola at her building, parked the car and entered the waiting area of the office.

"Detective Bruno! What a pleasant surprise. That is, I hope pleasant."

"Hello, Attorney DiAngelo. Nothing unpleasant I am sure. Can we have a minute of your time?"

"Come on in. Did they offer you coffee or water?"

"I think she is getting us one each, thank you."

We settled into my office.

"What do I owe the pleasure of this visit and who is the new partner?"

"Detective Villalpando. He replaced O'Malley. You remember him."

"As though my life depended on it, which it did, only the wrong way. But same question, why the visit?"

"The PLCB calls the department every time any application for a license is received that they think may be of interest to us. You sent one regarding an after hours in New Ken. The club has some names on the membership that were of interest to the department."

"But you're in homicide. Why are you concerned over a club license, and, in another county at that?"

"You remember the shotgun killing of Alphonse?"

"I do, why?"

"He was the doorman of the Aloysius club. Some of the members of the Aloysius are members or on the board of this application as well. Since he was a resident of Allegheny County, both counties are interested in what is going on and what went down in that instance."

"I still don't understand."

"After hours competition can be very competitive. Downright deadly."

"I still don't see what that has to do with an application for a license."

"I realize that you have to make a living, Counselor, and that you perform services to clients that you represent. We also realize that sometimes the people that you represent are not always thought to be people with the cleanest criminal records. We have sources of information regarding the people most interested in opening this club. We also know that the people who were in charge of the Aloysius may have some interest in this club one way or another."

"How does that go, 'one way or another'?"

"They may not want it to open as it may be competition."

"In another county? About an hour away from Pittsburgh?"

"If the person running it can call and request attention then it might be considered not a request but an order. If that order isn't obeyed, maybe we have more ugly results."

"That's a real stretch, don't you think?"

"Do you? Remember, we're talking about money and a place to show income. That keeps the IRS and the Feds away. Couldn't get any more serious than that, wouldn't you agree?"

"I think you're reaching, but, hey, it fills up your workday. Same question though, why come to me?"

"Pretty much as a courtesy to let you know that we may be filing a protest to the liquor license application based on the credibility of the club. Also, if you can help us to get any ideas on the Alphonse matter. No names, but ideas."

"You think that they have the same guys from Pittsburgh that went to Vegas for Bugsy Siegel? They're all dead and buried. And not under a fountain like the other guy from West Mifflin."

"I think they may be people that your clients may want you to tell us about as it may help your clients stay alive and in business."

"My compliments. That's pretty smooth. Regrettably, I don't have any ideas that I can share with you and I'm not sure that I could ethically provide anything anyhow. Tell you what though, let me talk to my clients and tell them I talked to you and what you were asking. Let me see what they think of your idea. Also, can I tell them that if they provide any info to you that you will refrain from filing any objections to the license application and will make sure that your counterparts in the other county do the same?"

"I don't know that I can do that."

"Then what incentive are you making for any help? We can wait until the hearing on the objection and I can promise you that all the members are clean. We did a BCI check on all of them before we filed the application just to avoid what you are suggesting. This isn't the first license app that this office has done and we looked ahead to any possible objection. Not perfect, but we try to make sure that all bases are covered. Now, what can you do for me that I should talk to my clean upstanding clients on your behalf?"

"You know the club might get visited to be sure that they close on time and that no people of questionable backgrounds frequent the club."

"Why try to muscle me? I have been very up front with you. Why try to get tough?"

"Sorry, I guess I was reaching a little. Tell you what, your offer before wasn't unreasonable. Let me consider what you said and maybe we can do each other some good."

"Ok, that's enough for one day. Your new partner hasn't said a word. What's up?"

"He just got promoted, still learning. Doesn't want to embarrass either of us."

"I'll be in touch if I don't forget. Stay well. Nice meeting your partner. Try to keep this one out of jail."

Since I was dealing with lawmen, I figured I might as well keep on going.

"United States Attorney's Office, how may I help you?"

"This is Attorney Lou DiAngelo from Pittsburgh. Your office has issued a grand jury subpoena to a client of mine and I would like to find out what is really going on."

"Thank you, I'll switch you over to Attorney Robinson who is working on the Grand Jury information. Hold the line, please."

"Hello, Attorney Robinson here."

"Mr. Robinson, this is Attorney Lou DiAngelo in Pittsburgh. I have two people that have alerted me that they have been subpoenaed to appear before your grand jury proceedings. One is Attorney Bergman from New York and the other is Mr. Parks who lives in Pittsburgh. I am wondering if we can get to the heart of what is going on here. Mr. Bergman was acting on behalf of my client to try to secure a piece of property that Mr. Parks owned and Mr. Parks was an absentee landlord in a bad rental situation. Are they really needed at your place?"

"I'm sorry, I haven't reviewed the persons you mention. The subpoena has them coming in when?"

"Not for another two weeks."

"A lifetime away. What were you suggesting?"

"Well, Attorney Bergman has no interest in the property, he was doing me a favor and performing an Action in Ejectment to get the property secured and have my client be able to unload it. He did some legal work and that was it."

"And Mr. Parks?"

"He had an investment property that wasn't turning out to be profitable."

"Does he have any idea of the people who lived there?"

"You know, now that you mention it, I really can't answer that. I was under the impression that he didn't, but I never really asked him. Would that be what you were looking to find out?"

"I'm not sure either. I am sure that we will want information on who was there but I will have to review the history of the file. I am in the middle of interrogating witnesses on drug and prostitution activity. They are from around the country as you might guess. I'll tell you what, see what Mr. Parks can tell you about the people that lived there, and let me review my file. Maybe we can help each other get the result that we both want and no harm done."

"Sounds like a deal. Let me give you my phone number and email information and I will get back to you within a week."

"Ok, sounds like a plan."

"Thank you."

That ended with some promise. Now I looked for my mail when Sherry buzzed.

"Allana is here. She says she has an appointment."

"Oh, shit, yes, she does. I'll be right with her." I straightened up the office and ushered her in.

She had on a silky top and skirt. They each barely covered the essentials. All the better to get better tips. She sat down and seemed a little nervous.

"May I smoke?"

"Sure. Ashtrays are on the desk."

"You don't mind?"

"I don't recommend cigarettes, but it's your life."

"Cigars that you smoke any better?"

"Let's just say there is nothing favorably reported that you can say about the use of tobacco. I read a book about cancer, <u>The Emperor of Maladies</u>, I think it was. Had a chapter about tobacco. Not good. But with cigars most of us don't inhale which reduces the danger of lung cancer. We only have to deal with throat, mouth, etc. But that's not why you're here. Shall we get on with it?"

"Sure, thanks. I'm glad you could and would see me. You realize that I have children but you don't know that their father is Danny Deacon and he has been calling and threatening me about their custody. He wants to see them every chance that he can and when I go to work."

"How old are they?"

"Twelve and fifteen."

"You have kids that old? You're practically a baby yourself."

"You're very kind but I got an early start in life. Those were the days of clubs and bar hopping and casual relationships that sometimes turned out to be serious."

"Especially with him."

"Well, he was exciting and we did have lots of fun, but then one day you find out that you have to now be an adult as you have responsibilities beyond just having fun."

"Does he pay any support?"

"How can he? He's on work release and was hurt in a motorcycle crash a couple of years ago. I think he gets disability and maybe social security."

We discussed all the pros and cons and what was needed to be done and she was apparently satisfied with the proposed plan that was outlined regarding setting up partial custody.

"How much will you need?"

"You get right to it, don't you?"

"I know you have to be paid. I just need to know how much."

"Depending on how much work we have to do, you can be sure that it will probably run at least $2,500."

She pulled her bag up from the floor and counted out 25 one hundred dollar bills to my almost open-mouthed surprise.

"How soon can you get started?"

"Right now. My secretary will have some papers for you to sign and then we will make contact. You are sure of the address for him, right?"

"If he's not there when the PO comes around, his address will be the State Correctional."

"Ok, we'll get rolling."

"Thanks," and she pecked me on the cheek and swung out the door. Probably does better that I thought at Bob's Garage and still looked young enough to be carded at any bar.

My secretary buzzed. "Tony's on the phone. Sounds like he's very upset, not angry upset."

"Tony, what's up?"

"It's Sam. He's dead. Shot in the face. They found him last night. I have to meet with you. How about tonight, as soon as possible?"

"Ok, where?"

"Franco's in Harmarville. About seven thirty. Oh my God. I'm sorry, I have to hang up."

That was the end. Now what, I wondered?

I took a break from the research and preparations as I looked at my watch. It was about time to head to Bloomfield to meet Steve for lunch. I closed out the issues that I was working on and headed for the door. Traffic was not overly bad. Got a parking spot reasonably close and I went to the bar. Chrissie was working the bar and made me a Manhattan. Caesar was working the door and Alex had on an apron.

"What's the matter, can't afford a good cook and Dutch walked on you?"

"Every now and again I get inspired. What brings you out our way?"

"Have a guy that wants to meet me, but not in town. What's on for today?"

"You're in luck. Have some fresh tripe sautéed in a red sauce and we have baby back ribs."

"You know I'm a sucker for tripe. How's everything else going?"

"Hey, I'm healthy and business is doing good enough."

Steve then appeared.

"Hello, Counselor. Thanks for being on time."

We moved over to one of the tables in the bar. The bar had a few people having a conversation so that we knew we would have enough quiet.

"You know I have a lot of hope now that you are trying to get me back to work with the Pardon and everything. I needed to see you as the old guy is getting his ear filled and I'm not sure if it will affect you or not. You know Sam's death is still very quiet and I am a little nervous as there is usually a body that turns up somewhere after a hit like that. How are you getting along with the old man?"

"Fine so far as I can see."

"Be careful, Counselor, something ain't right."

"What do you think it might be, Steve?"

"There are a lot of new faces. Guys that don't get introduced and I know they aren't made men. They might be recruits but I don't know who sponsored them. Just ain't normal. But anyway, I needed to talk to you about my pardon. I got a job with a car dealer on the Parkway East as a consultant. I assist in preparing the cars for delivery. I can't do sales as I can't get a salesman license with a record. He needs to talk to you to see how I can get paid and whether you can set up a contract basis so that I am not on his payroll."

"That's the right approach. He gives you employment as an entrepreneur and doesn't have to carry you on the books. He gets no grief and no obligations."

"Hey, entrepreneur! I like that word. Did I say it right?"

"Yes, you did. Now you are promoted to be a working class stiff."

"Did I do good?"

"You did fine. Anything else?"

"I still got a feeling we haven't heard the last of the case on Sam's death. I'm telling you."

"Sometimes the best solution is to do nothing. More killing causes more heat and the one thing none of your friends needs is more heat."

"Whatever you say. I'm just telling you, watch your step."

"Thanks, Steve. Your pardon hearing is coming up in a little while. I'll be in touch."

I left and headed back to the office.

CHAPTER FIVE

The rest of the afternoon was fortunately court appearances for Judge Bartolomeo to appoint me the Master in the Partition Hearing, and Motion for Discovery in a domestic case. After that, I prepared the Application for a Governor's Pardon, did some paperwork and odds and ends. Lola called but I couldn't have drinks or dinner and certainly couldn't have her at Franco's with me.

I closed up late and started to the meeting. I wasn't sure what the deal was with the meeting but it was one that had to be kept.

The ride was quick as the rush hour was over. I took Route 28 to the Harmarville exit and made my way up the road to the lot. Weekday nights should be a smaller crowd but there were enough cars to have it appear that they were doing business. Lori was behind the bar. Her hair was down and looked like a shampoo commercial for a lustrous brown. She smiled her usual bright smile that lights up the place as she reached behind her while saying hello.

"Macallan?"

"Thank you, yes."

"You are expected, you know."

"Am I late?"

"There are some people in the back dining room that asked that you be sent back as soon as you arrive. I can bring the drink back. They also asked if we could keep the other table back there empty. Not too much trouble tonight. We probably won't need the extra tables."

I walked back and Tony jumped up and rushed over, grabbing me and hugging me.

"My friend, my friend, I knew I could count on you. Come over and meet Billy, Michael and Zartan."

I had met Billy and Michael before. Billy was the serious one. Michael was merely a gofer. Zartan, I wasn't sure about. Having been with him before, he never made much of an impression. He always seemed to be thinking of someone or something else when he was talking to you. Billy stood and we shook hands.

"I remember Attorney DiAngelo. We had some issues he had to straighten out for us in Florida. We were all together in Fort Lauderdale and West Palm. That cowboy from Philadelphia was down there for a wedding. Nicodeme, Nicodeme, what's his name?"

"Scarfo."

"Yeah, that's right. That was a hot time."

That was before everything got crazy. They were having a good time. They didn't do anything wrong. Not down there anyhow. It was a wedding. One of his kids, I think. Nobody was going to act up at that event or then there would have been serious consequences. But it was a good time.

"Were you invited to the wedding, Counselor?"

"No. I just happened to be there. We wound up having some drinks at the outdoor bar. The Tiki Bar, Tiki Hut, something like that? I saw that they were serious guys so I bought them all a drink. Also, to be safe."

"Ok, enough already. You guys can get familiar later. We got some things to discuss. I asked the counselor here because with Sam gone we need some direction and we've got to make sure that we don't lose any type of legal position or whatever. Now, Counselor, I need you to tell us what happens now that Sam is dead and what we do since he was the manager and owner of the license. What do you think, Luigi?"

"Well, you're going to need someone to replace him as the manager. That can be done with a form application. They will do a background check and investigate the person so they have got to be clean. It can be anybody you want. If you go to a new owner then it has to be a transfer with a complete investigation. It might be better to have an heir, like Sam's wife or daughter."

"Hey, that's right up our alley. Tony is married to Sam's daughter. If she takes it then we have what we need. How about that, Tony?"

"I don't know. I'll have to ask her if she feels comfortable with it. Also, I have to be sure that it's ok with the old guy because I don't want him to think I'm trying to make a move."

"What do you think, Counselor?"

"It can be done. It will be a lot less headache and paperwork, and she has no history to cause trouble. It will probably work."

"I think we take it to the number one and try it out."

The meeting went pretty well from that point on as they saw an opening to get what they all wanted. It crossed my mind, 'Why all the people from Hazelton, West Palm, Wilkes-Barre/Scranton for a simple club license transfer? Why an elephant gun to kill a fly?'

The meeting ended with offers for dinner, but I had put up with enough for the night. The day had been long enough. Time to head home. Their discussion continued as I left.

I got home, pulled in, closed the garage door and to the upstairs bar. Pulled out the Macallan 30 year old. Two fingers worth were deserved. I thought about Billy and Michael, I hadn't seen them since Filo's kid's birthday, I think. That was a long time ago. Billy had beaten some federal charges since then. Michael had a pending divorce, seems like he was doing a lot of personnel work at the office, and one secretary in particular. Zartan was an ever elusive figure. Not sure why he was there, haven't seen him since West Palm in Florida. Something was under the surface. Maybe tomorrow. Off to bed. I wondered what tomorrow would look like. What about the old man, would we ever meet?

CHAPTER SIX

"Mr. DiAngelo?"

"Yes."

"Rosa on the phone."

"Thank you."

"Louie, sweetheart, I hear you got a call from Dukie."

"Yes, I did, why?"

"Because Joe Chic is in town and he is interested in that case as well. The young guy will call you as soon as I hang up. He's going to want to meet with you. After you meet with him, Joe Chic, Freddie from the clerk's office and my husband are going to want to meet with you about the case."

"This is the guy with the marijuana and the receiving stolen property, right?"

"That's right. You know the state's attorney and the district attorney are all in on this."

"Over this little beef?"

"You didn't hear about the other things?"

"No."

"He'll call you."

The phone was still warm when I was buzzed.

"A Mr. Mirage on the line. Says Rosa told him to call."

"Hello, Attorney DiAngelo here, how may I help you?"

"My name is Salvatore Mirage. Rosa told me to call you. Can I come and see you?"

"When?"

"Right now. I'm two blocks away."

"You're in luck. My office is empty. Come on."

He was there in less than ten minutes. He had that wannabe look about him. He was checking out my employees and viewing them just short of a leer. He was smiling that greaser smile that I hated.

"Mr. Mirage, come on in."

He had a coffee in his hand and he sat down. Placed the coffee on my desk and sat in the hard chair nearest my desk.

"You got all shades of beauty out there. Light skinned, dark. All easy on the eyes. Do you spend many nights working late?"

"There is a serving tray beside you. Put your coffee on that please, and off my desk. My working hours are my business, and my staff are my staff because they can do their job. Now, suppose you allow me to do my job. Why the anxious need to see me?"

"Hey, I didn't come here to be insulted. I don't need some shit attorney going high on the hog on me. I don't need you. Do you remember who I am? You handled my divorce."

"Quite frankly, no and I also don't give a fuck. You were sent here and I was asked to see you. If you want to leave, be my guest. I will be happy to call Rosa and tell her that you didn't really think you needed me and that you left. I'll tell her that you figured that she must have made a mistake and that Joe Chic should send you elsewhere. Is that what you want? Besides, I'm supposed to meet a Mr. Dellacroce, not Mirage."

"Well, uh, I'm not … I… listen, I don't mean nothin'. I just ain't used to being told what I can do and… ok, ok, maybe I shouldn't made that crack about the dames. Can we start over?"

"How about your name, date of birth, mailing address and did you bring any papers with you?"

"I brung what I have but I got to tell you some other stuff. You know about the stolen property and the marijuana but I got a notice that they are filing other charges, as well. I got pinched picking up some numbers and sports bets by the state and the county has an arrest warrant because of a gun they found in my house that was used in a shooting."

"Were you involved in the shooting?"

"I ain't at liberty to say."

"Was anybody killed?"

"No."

"Was there a reason for the shooting?"

"I ain't at liberty to say."

"Was it your gun?"

"I ain't at liberty to say."

"How do you expect me to defend you if you aren't going to tell me anything?"

"Just because I'm all jammed up don't mean that I can talk. Even to my attorney. Listen, you will be paid real good, and all you got to do is your job as an attorney. I was told to come here so I'm here. After you meet with the guys tonight, you'll understand. Please forgive me, but I gotta do what I gotta do. I know it's crazy but that's how it is."

"I'm going to need about $20,000 considering the charges. That figure may grow as well."

"We'll talk about that after you have your meet. I apologize for whatever I did here, but I am told what to do and then I do it."

"Ok, I suppose we'll talk more after the meeting tonight. Maybe how you are Dellacroce and Mirage?"

"My uncle was a cop and my father did a stretch. Neither helped me in my profession."

With that we parted company.

Funny. He's the kind of guy that makes you feel that you need to bathe after you are with him, but you somehow pity his type as well, as he doesn't know any better and never will. This was the guy that Duke had called and said was Dellacroce. Why did we get to Mr. Mirage? All for a later day.

"Mr. Bergman on the phone."

"Bruce, how are you?"

"You tell me. What's with the subpoena?"

"The U.S. Attorney is calling it off for you. I have yet to get the confirming call, but it looks lead pipe."

"Says you. I hope you're right. My partners don't need newspapers calling."

"Believe me, it's over, I'm sure."

"You know some other agents called, as well. They were with Immigration. What the hell was going on up there?"

"I really don't know but will try to find out if you think it's important."

"Maybe nothing. A lot of border crossings so maybe they thought it was like a safe house."

"Maybe it was, but I will try to find out."

"Keep me posted and I don't have to schedule a grand jury, right?"

"Guaranteed."

"I'll bet. Ok, thanks."

CHAPTER SEVEN

The streets were crowded around the Amen Funeral Home. I looked over the cars and didn't see any heads. I was sure that there were agents around somewhere. Possibly because so many of the stiffs came to this place, the feds probably bought a building as a surveillance site. I don't think they could have ever rented a room and kept it a secret as they would have to pay rent to somebody and, almost surely, word would get out. The place was up to full operation with door handlers and greeters and staff people ready to perform whatever tasks that might be required. Herb Amen was on hand and moving about.

"Counselor, how are you?"

"Couldn't be better."

He felt my pulse with his left hand as he shook my hand.

"Still a strong pulse, too soon."

"Don't rush me, Herb. How's everything going?"

"Closed casket. Face was in pretty bad shape. Intentional wound to cause the closure. Only so much a guy can do. Better to have it closed."

"How's the wife taking it?"

"Pretty solid. The cummati isn't doing as well. But his daughter is the maddest. If she were a guy, I'm sure there would be a contract out already and a major war. She may have to lean on her husband, Tony, for that but that's for another day. When Fio got killed, there was no vendetta by his brothers or family since the shooter was that nutty Nickie. He went to the can for life and no financial reason to kill him as he was a looney anyhow. Oh well, it's good for my business if they get mad."

I went into the viewing room and moved through the line. All the troops were there as required. When I got to the bier, I paid my respects to the wife and daughter and Tony. Herbie was right, you could feel the heat coming from the daughter. Tony was as gracious and cordial as possible under the circumstances. I didn't see the old man, but that didn't mean anything as he would probably arrange a private meeting at the funeral parlor and offer his financial support and whatever else for the wake. The flowers were from the floor to the ceiling in every room in the place. Of all people, Joe Chic was nearby and he made it a point to get to me.

"Eight o'clock, we can meet downstairs. Frank Simeone and Freddie are on their way. Save you a trip and kill two birds with, oh, let me take that back, save you a trip and some time, ok, Counselor?"

"Sure, that will work. What better place than with some stiffs on ice."

His eyes went wide.

"You think there will be bodies down there?"

"That's where they prepare them."

"Oh, Christ, let me ask Herb if there are any. Oh Jesus!"

"What's to worry? They're past spreading stories."

"You got some mouth, you, but I guess you're right. It's still too creepy. Let me check."

For an old timer, I was surprised at his reaction. He was well known and I'm certain that he was made and not on the lower rung. He commanded respect and deference from Sam, Tony, Michael but not Billy as I recall. The cast of characters was getting interesting. I watched him grab Herb and then he nodded to me a look of relief, no prospects downstairs it appeared.

I spent some time chatting with guys from the avenue. I noticed Sam's mistress or cummati as the Italians called the girlfriend and she had on a wig and was covered up pretty well. She didn't look the same as she always did out of respect, I suppose, for the family and to avoid being recognized. Sam's widow didn't know about her but I wasn't sure about the daughter.

"Mr. DiAngelo, how you a-doing?"

"Excuse me? Oh, my goodness, Mrs. Cuccinetti, you caught me by surprise. How are you? I forgot this is still your neighborhood, isn't it?"

"That's a-right and I used to go to a-church with his mother. She was a nice lady too."

"How is everything for you?"

"Better since you fix up-a my son's things, what-a you call?"

"His estate. But that was nothing. The other stuff was tougher, but, thanks to police, that all got cleared up without too much trouble."

"I'm-a need to talk-a to you again and when you get-a the time."

"Okay. I still have your number. How about I call you next week?"

"That-a be nice. I make you something to eat, maybe ok?"

"Maybe ok, for sure."

I wandered off and mingled with all the familiar faces when I saw Joe Chic with the other two and he motioned toward the door going downstairs. We all made our way down to a room in the rear that appeared to be a small office. Chic spoke up.

"We got the counselor here and now we got to figure out what is going on. Just so you know, Lou, Fred thinks he can get us to a favorable courtroom where our kid won't get beat up."

"Whoa! I don't want to hear any talk like that!"

"Relax, we aren't getting you involved in anything, we're just telling you because we need you to be gentle on your fee especially if we are helping you."

"If you think you're going to get help on these charges, you're nuts. And I am not reducing my fee for this case. It's going to take a lot of time in preparing and then the trial. I am curious what the interest is with all you guys, but I'm not going to ask because I really don't want to know. I also am curious why he has a different name and why he is so closed mouth with me but, once again, I am not going to ask. The marijuana, the stolen property, the bookmaking are all well and good and if he has a fairly clean record he should get no jail time or very little, but a gun charge and if somebody was hurt, changes the entire outlook. Unless he has some great alibi, he is looking at serious trouble. I don't care who you think you know."

"You will represent him though, won't you?"

"I wasn't particularly taken with him when I met him but he is entitled to the best that I can do for him. I'll take the case but he has to come up with the fee before I do anything."

"How about if he gives you half and I guarantee the balance."

"If you guarantee that means I can look to you for the money."

"That's right."

"I want you to be sure you know what you're saying and you're saying it in front of these two guys as well. You guys understand what he is saying?"

"We all know. We all agree you'll be taken care of."

"Then, on that note, that you all guaranteed the money, I am leaving and don't want to hear anything else except the check hit the desk and his phone call. Good night."

CHAPTER EIGHT

The settlement check had arrived. All those zeroes. I instructed the staff regarding the next steps and dictated the cover letter. Instructions were to overnight with a return overnight envelope, stamped the check for deposit in our IOLTA account and the documents in need of the signature of the widow. Fee would be reduced to thirty five percent even though we had tried the case and were at closing. All the expenses had been paid by the widow already and it wasn't much of a liability question, merely a question of dollars.

Jennifer buzzed me, "A Miss Allana in the phone."

"Thank you."

"Hello, this is Attorney DiAngelo."

"Good morning. Thank you for taking the call. Do you know a Mr. Mirage?"

"Why?"

"There was some talk at the bar last night and I happened to overhear your name and the name of a Mr. Mirage in the same conversation. The people talking had accents and didn't always speak in English. There was something about a whiskey deal as well. Really seemed like something so I thought you might be interested. I also needed to talk to you about the custody hearing. My ex called real upset and threatening to take steps if I didn't wise up, as he says. I'm not sure what I should do but I think you and I know what he means."

"Is he still in touch with any of his old cronies?"

"I'm not sure. Why?"

"If we need to we can try to have you protected from him and any of his associates by a court order."

"Do you think that will help?"

"It usually does. I haven't heard from his attorney yet regarding the Petition we filed. Maybe I can call him? Do you know or did he say if he had an attorney?"

"He was complaining that he didn't have any money to afford an attorney and the legal aid attorneys don't have enough staff to take domestic cases unless they are abuse cases. I guess that means that you can call him."

She gave me his number, then I asked about the conversation last night.

"They were two big men and then another one who was dressed like in the gangster movies. He wasn't real big. I think they called him Sally. Why a girl's name, I was wondering."

"It's short for Salvatore. Ok, I'll call your husband and then we'll see if he and I can get some resolution of any differences. Didn't your husband used to hang out at Tigano's?"

"That's where I met him, curse the day."

"Hey, he gave you beautiful children. Look at the good side."

We ended our conversation and I started to work on the Partition case.

"Mr. DiAngelo, Tony on the phone."

"Hello, Tony, how can I help you?"

"Maybe I can help you. The old guy wants to have you over this weekend. Whatever night is good for you he wants to set up a dinner at the club. We had a visit from the inspector. He said the report he is sending is fine and he gave us approval to start operating on a temporary license until the final comes in to us. What's good for you?"

"How about Saturday?"

"That'll work. What time?"

"Is eight or eight thirty okay?"

"We'll be ready for you. You, your date and any friends. Let me know if anybody you bring has any diet problems like allergic to shellfish or vegetarians or anything like that?"

"Anybody I bring?"

"Yeah, bring whoever the fuck you want. The old guy is thrilled."

"Okay, make it six. This way I have backup."

"You're so crazy. We'll set a table for ten in case you think you really need help. You know even ten wouldn't cause us too much trouble. See you Saturday."

Back to the Partition case. Looked like all was in order. Now to schedule the preliminary meeting with counsel. Would have to call John Tunney and Mark Pukalski to see what their schedules were like. John was an old time practitioner. He was pretty much a fake and a snake. He came off like a goody two shoes but was as devious as they come. Pukalski was a good kid and no problems with his legal talent. I knew what to expect at any hearing. Both were going to see what their calendars could do two weeks from the day I called.

"Mr. DiAngelo, Lola on the blinker."

"Hello, wonderful lady."

"If I were so wonderful, I might get a call once in a while."

"How about in a little while or do want to settle for only once?"

"Last time you were better than that, twice as I recall. But enough about your inadequacies, how about dinner some time before I forget what it is all about."

"Let's go see Jimmy at Girasole's. I think they have that singer there tonight as well."

"Anywhere so long as I am served and don't have to order take out or cook."

"A deal. I'll pick you up at 7:30. Hey, I have to go to a dinner Saturday. Available?"

"Try to stop me from being there. By the way, where is there?"

"A club out in New Ken. Have any ideas who we might bring along?"

"Excuse me? What are you asking me?"

"I can bring anybody I want for reinforcements. We have a table for ten."

"Dear God, it's a bacchanal. I would suggest Leo and Carole Rae, and Chinky and Marge but it's your party. You want any of my family?"

"No."

"Hey!"

"I accepted your suggestions. That's enough folks for one night. See you later."

I then did some research on the custody matter and dialed the phone number for Deacon.

"Hello."

"Hello, this is Attorney DiAngelo. Are you busy, or can we speak about the custody matter, or do have an attorney with whom I should have this conversation?"

"Hey, Lou, you don't have to get formal with me. Don't you remember me from Tigano's, I remember you. I used to run with Billy and Inky. I was the one with the link chains around my neck. That's when I was a lot younger. Then again, so were you."

"You know what, I think I do remember you. You drank that sangria or whatever."

"Yeah, that's me. Why are you calling me?"

"I want to see if I can help keep you from coming to town and if we can get some work out done on the custody thing."

"She doesn't want my kids to see me. I'm a bad influence. I got arrested and convicted so now I'm shit, is that it?"

"No, that's not it at all. She only wants to have a set pattern for custody and a definite arrangement. It's not set in cement but she needs to have some guidelines as to partial custody and visitation."

"And money for support, I guess too."

"Can you pay anything for support?"

"I'm on disability, but I'm not a stiff. I can try to make some effort."

"That isn't really her concern. I can suggest some guidelines like every other weekend and one night during the off week. Summer you get expanded time when they are out of school. Stuff like that. Why don't I send you a proposal? You can have your attorney look at it and review and then we can decide."

"I can't afford an attorney, but I know you and I know what I want to try to do. I'm sure we can figure it out. She's paying you, right? I mean you ain't getting cozy for the fee, are you?"

"Never happen. Not in anybody's lifetime."

"She knows how to get her way, I can tell you. I've seen her in action."

"I'll bet. At any rate, I'll get something in the mail to you and we'll go from there."

"Okay, Lou. I'm hoping you won't try to screw me. I'm trying to do the right thing."

We ended on a good note. I had Jennifer run off a form agreement for partial custody and visitation.

"Mr. DiAngelo, the Assistant U.S. Attorney from New York."

"Send it through."

"Mr. Robinson, I presume."

"And Mr. Victor and Mr. Cohen are here with me as well."

"Hey, that's not fair to outnumber me three to one and on my tax dollars to boot."

"More of a courtesy call and an inquiry, Attorney DiAngelo. Mr. Victor is from Immigration and M. Cohen is with Justice assigned to State. We are trying to find out if Mr. Parks or Mr. Bergman had any knowledge of the people that lived in the upstate New York residence."

"I'm sure that Attorney Bergman had no knowledge of the people and the best that I can recall Mr. Parks had a real estate agent managing the property. I know this is almost redundant, but did you speak to the agent?"

"She's dead. And dead under mysterious circumstances."

"How so?"

"Drowned in a creek relatively near the property. The creek is not easily accessible from the residence so it appears that she had to make an effort to get there. Either she was taken there or was trying to get away from whoever was in the residence."

"As I recall, the occupants were shooting at the process server in the Ejectment Action. Attorney Bergman had to have the sheriff or local police assist in service. Then again, if I recall, the residents abandoned the property before the next step occurred. I think they took everything with them as well."

"Not quite everything. There were a couple of very sophisticated forged passports found in the basement. Did anybody you know have any contact with the residents at all?"

"Well, I know that Attorney Bergman did not. I will check with Mr. Parks and I'll let you know."

"I appreciate your cooperation, Attorney DiAngelo. So that you know, neither Mr. Parks nor Mr. Bergman will have to appear. We have postponed their appearance for now."

"Thank you. I'll see what I can find out for you. How about that, I'm helping the prosecution."

CHAPTER NINE

"Are you ready to get the kid off, Counselor?"

"You must be crazy. I never expect to get all the charges thrown out. I wasn't at his preliminary and you guys are talking about how this is going to be a walk in the park. From growing marijuana to receiving stolen property, operating an illegal book and finally possible attempted homicide as the gun they found in his home was used in a shooting. What do you expect Eagle Scout Badge of Honor or Presidential Award for Citizenship?"

"I mean do you have any idea about how you are going to get him off."

"Not in the least. I will need to see what they can present as evidence. Do you have any idea what or who we can present?"

"We can present Joe Storio and Lou Candido as character witnesses."

"For this character? From those characters? Storio is a pretty faced council member and Candido is a constable with no apparent good history. You guys kill me. Besides the money you paid me, there is no reason that I would be here. He's a piece of shit and you know it. He thinks he's New York but he's strictly farm country. Look, I am in this because of Joe Chic and that's it."

"The $20,000 probably had something to do with it. Don't forget. Are you going to pick a jury?"

"Not with the evidence that I know about. And you guys think you are in front of the right guy so why allow a jury to get the judge off the hook. I don't believe any of that crap but you go on believing what you want. You have guys like Freddy telling you that they can help. They are so full of baloney, it makes me laugh. They are, like him, snake oil salesmen. If it turns out right, they did it. If wrong, they don't know why the judge did it. Because the judge will be doing his job, that's why."

Judge Romannelo came out on the bench. Across the table from me were three police officers from different police forces: County, Township and State. There were also three prosecutors. One from the Attorney General's office, two from the District Attorney's office. I knew the ones from the DA's office. Marilyn was a tough prosecutor with no quarter given. Jimmy was easy going, sort of laid back, but always ready with his case and wouldn't give up on a point when he thought he was right. On the other hand, he would not go for any out of left field criminal counts that didn't measure up.

"Is the prosecution ready?"

"Yes, your Honor."

"Mr. DiAngelo, ready to proceed?"

"Yes, your Honor."

"Bring the Defendant forward."

We approached the microphones and the judge read him all the information against him, his right to a jury trial and all the other pro forma information.

The trial began. The first three witnesses were all the police officers who reported all that they had observed and reports that they took. Not a bad start for the weasel next to me as they all dealt with the minor offenses, how they saw the marijuana plants, saw the stolen merchandise, followed him to a few bars where he picked up sports bets. Nothing on the pistol or shooting before lunch.

We broke for lunch and went separate ways for lunch. I felt like the William Penn where Santiago got me down and out in good time. I started for the street when I saw Filo and Cy.

"Hey! What are you guys doing in town?"

"We're not allowed to be in Pittsburgh?"

"You know what I mean."

"We hear there is an interesting case across the street."

"You don't mean…"

"Counselor, you get all the goodies, don't you?"

"And you still don't know who was in the car with him when the shooting occurred, do you?"

"What the…"

"Easy, Counselor. He is nothing."

"Z and JB and Joe Chic will make sure the name never comes out."

"The old man wouldn't like it."

"I have no idea who or what and it is none of my business at this point. I am trying to defend a case where all the evidence is on their side."

"Everybody knows that you'll do your best. Sometimes even the best isn't good enough."

Son of a bitch. It dawns on me. I'm expected to lose the case! It now appears that maybe they will want the kid to get convicted and they were trying to impress the judge to find him guilty. Why? Possibly to get him to roll over and rat out whoever was in the car or at the scene or whatever in order to get that person out of their way or harm's way or any way. I'll be damned.

"Are you in town for any particular reason?"

"We like the food and the scenery. And the whiskey. We'll see you later on at the club on Saturday."

"You know about that?"

"Talk to you later, Counselor. Keep up the good work."

Back to court. The prosecution now called their witnesses regarding the shooting.

"Hi, Lou."

"Hi, Danny. What are you doing here?"

"I am a witness for the prosecution about the shooting. I was at the scene when it all went down."

With that he proceeded to the witness chair, was sworn and began relating how Mr. Mirage encountered several individuals and that a shooting had taken place. No one was wounded so far as he could tell. He saw clearly the face of Mr. Mirage from an elevated porch along Paulson Avenue, just beyond Paulson Field and looking down on the scene about thirty yards away. Danny works for the Clerk of Courts, Criminal Division and is the First Assistant. A tall, African American with a striking resemblance to Floyd Patterson. He is a stand up guy who is always ready to help and knows his job. Not only that, but he made a terribly credible witness.

I went through the usual cross examination, lighting, time of day, eyesight, etc., but it was purely an exercise and he wasn't moved at all. He was polished and certain of all his testimony.

When excused, he passed by me and apologized, as he knew that his testimony wasn't what I wanted to hear but it was what it was.

The court recessed for the day. We left the courtroom and the three people that brought Mirage to me were waiting.

"How did it go, Counselor?"

"Not good at all. If I were the judge, and this kid were my friend, he would still be guilty on all counts and no mitigation. He couldn't have done worse if he had tried. Broad daylight, populated area. I haven't been given a reason for what happened such as self-defense or some other reason why the shooting took place. The only good thing is that no body or victim has been produced. Then it would be a homicide case. Discharging a firearm and that calls for three prosecuting attorneys? I don't need to know what else. I have no idea what you guys expect, but it better not be anything good."

Mr. Mirage then chimed in, "Don't worry, Cump, everything will be fine."

"You're telling me not to worry, you're the guy in trouble, Mr. Mirage. This witness is a well-known court employee. Didn't you hear him when he testified as to his employment? The judges all know him and rely on him. They aren't going to doubt him, nor are they going to believe you before him if you even get to testify. Can you give me anything to present?"

"Don't worry, there's more to this than you know. I'll be okay."

I couldn't believe what I was hearing. If he wasn't worried, why was I getting worked up and anxious? In spite of all of my suspicions on this case from all angles, I was still the defense attorney and this thug, as much as I didn't like him, was my responsibility. And as my profession had ingrained in me, he should be able to depend on me. I've known all types of people involved in activities not exactly legal, but there are different degrees of whether they are likable or not. This one was definitely on my 'don't come back' list. As a matter of fact, he was brought to me. We parted and I went back to the office. The prosecution would probably wind up tomorrow.

A few phone messages for me to call back were on my desk.

"Tony, Attorney Lou DiAngelo."

"Hey, Luig. Thanks for calling back, how's the final approval coming?"

"If it's done, you should have it. I haven't seen my mail yet."

"I didn't see it at the club. In other words, if it's finally approved then they mail it?"

"They have to print it as well, but that's all on computer and shouldn't be a problem except at renewal time."

"Good, I have to see you as soon as you have time. Can I see you as soon as your case is over?"

"What case?"

"The shooting case with Mirage."

"How do you know about that case?"

"Not to worry, we hear many things."

Just what I needed, I thought, more cloak and dagger.

"I might be able to get to you by the end of the week. Can't it wait until Saturday night when I come for dinner?"

"I don't want to talk business at a party and where other people can hear. I know you understand."

"I'll see what I can do."

Returned a call to Allana on her custody matter. All was falling into place. Surprisingly, they are acting as adults over children that aren't babies anymore.

The Greek was advised that a hearing before the Pardon Board was scheduled for six weeks from now. He wanted to know if we could get it moved up. Everybody thinks their case is the most important. And it is, to them. But, the courts and hearing officers, etc., work at the best pace that they can go. Everybody wants to sue, or, get out of jail now, or justice immediately.

The most important call was next.

"Hello, calling me on my cell at work. Shame on you."

"I didn't want to waste the time if it wasn't you that answered."

"You got lucky."

"That's what I had in mind."

"Me, too. You've been busy and I've been lonely."

"I hope so. I don't want you to start looking elsewhere. I am about to wrap up. How does your evening look?"

"Like it was made for you."

"We haven't seen Jimmy Pi for a while. Feel like that ravioli with tomato cream sauce. I think I promised you Girasole's for dinner recently anyhow. May I pick you up at seven?"

"May I? Pick me up? You must be having a rough week with the over the top courtesy."

"If you only knew."

"Shall I pack a bag?"

"Sorry, I'm in trial and up to my ears with clients. Maybe after the case we go for a weekend somewhere. Mountaineer, D.C., New York? Think about it. Talk to you later."

"Attorney Eveready on the phone."

"Hello, Tom, how are you?"

"Great, Lou. Wanted to touch base with you. The case is coming around soon. What's the story on your end?"

"Let me call and find out. Can you give me a couple of days as I am in trial and a little frazzled."

"I know, I saw you in court today, that's what reminded me. I had a pretrial myself and had to be over there, when I saw you. I also saw some old timers outside your courtroom. Not a coincidence, I'll bet, let me know as soon as you can. Also, make sure your guy knows, no more muscle. My guy is a little worried that your guy will want to get even or maybe more ahead than he is at present."

"Consider it done."

No more, God, please. Off to home, shower, Girasole's and Lola, what could be better?

Thank you, God. I glanced through my mail. No protest had been filed and the license for the club had been approved. I owed Detective Bruno one now.

CHAPTER TEN

"Coompie, how are you? And the lovely lady still doesn't know any better, she's still with you."

"Hi, Jimmy."

"Good to see you, Pi. You have a lot of nerve suggesting my lady should go elsewhere. I might stop coming here."

"That would make the other customers happy. Then they could have conversations without trying to be heard over you."

"Hey, you're on a tear."

"Maybe. The LCB visited today. They've been visiting all the places because of a couple of incidents."

"Shootings on the South Side?"

"One happened up the street a couple of weeks ago, so the state and local police are cracking down on all the places a little. Not that we do anything wrong. Ours is more of a family place. No matter, it's still a headache. Let me get you seated."

"Thank you."

We ordered antipasto, Lola had the ravioli with tomato cream. I tried for the eggplant again as it was the best and lightest around, but he wouldn't sell it except as take out to me. I wasn't sure if he wanted me to leave or just order when I was too busy to appear personally. The place was crowded as always with people standing in line waiting. After a while he was able to sit.

"What do you know about Judges Pasquarelli and O'Hanlon?"

"Excuse me?"

"I just wanted to know if you know them."

"I know them both, why?"

"They've been coming in here recently, sit at the back table. She's a bit of a looker which he is not, but I had the feeling they are on the sneak."

"He's married. She is not. She's come a long way from the DA's office. Moved up the ladder to become a judge. Used to be a JP. Now a full-fledged judge and chasing after a Senior Judge. She doesn't care for me in the least as I know more than she would care for me to discuss."

"I heard your name mentioned, Counselor. Something about a criminal case down the hall from her courtroom."

"It seems everybody is hearing about that case."

"And some of the strength that was waiting outside the courtroom. Funny, probably because with all the LCB action, Joe Chic is in town, is strong on the bartenders' union, and showing an interest in this case. That doesn't make any rhyme or reason to me."

"Me either. Did her honor have any other comments about me that you heard?"

"No. But Pasquarelli was on your side. Said he knew you from his campaign days and that you did a decent job as an attorney, not a good job, mind you, a decent job."

"I heard you the first time."

We finished up, said our farewells to Patty, Jimmy's wife, who gets better looking everyday, probably because she works out daily. For a grandmother to look that good and be that sweet is major. Also not fair.

"Your place or mine?"

"I'm in the middle of a trial. I need to wrap up the night if you don't mind."

"I do mind and I thought I made my strictly dishonorable intentions clear when you suggested dinner. I could have skipped dinner and gone straight to the dessert tray."

She reached over and started to do things under the steering wheel that made me hopeless and helpless. We pulled up at her place.

"I promise I'll make it quick for you. You never could hold back anyhow."

We went into the house, as I would have been much less of a gentleman if I had declined to enter the house and its owner and she was as good as her word. I was not able to concentrate on the matter at hand since this case and all the intangibles start to creep into your thoughts and aren't conducive to manly performance. In spite of all the angst, she was a convincing partner that could make me forget impending atomic annihilation. Those legs, that tongue, the fact that we cared so intensely about each other gave me cause to forget all my problems and address the issue in front of me, making her feel satisfied. I did my best to get to all the parts that give sensation and sensational response. She responded enough times so that I felt that I wasn't taking advantage of her generosity and that we got to equal footing. We embraced for a while after all the bells and whistles and Fourth of July fireworks had gone off. I started to doze.

"I have to get going."

"I know. Thanks for not forgetting to stop in after dinner. I would have forgiven you since I understand how trials can be so demanding."

"Easy for you to say now, but I wasn't taking any chances. In addition, what have I got to complain about? So I lose a little sleep time. The guy is still going to jail anyhow."

"Please call me tomorrow. No phone call the day after makes one feel so cheap."

We both laughed at that remark as I headed for my car and sleep. I instinctively looked around her house because of past incidents, but saw nothing that seemed important. My mind raced about the trial, the judges mentioning my name, the fact that Joe Chic's presence was known and curious to more than just me. Tomorrow promised to be something. Maybe I should stop and say hello to a few judges, just to show my face to both and have them both thinking.

CHAPTER ELEVEN

The Courthouse was relatively busy with a lot of attorneys and faces that I knew for years with the usual smattering of new faces making old arguments that were new to them.

"Hi, Katy, how are you?"

"Hey, Lou, good to see you. Where have you been hiding?"

"Up on the fifth floor, in a trial. Is Judge Pasquarelli in?"

"Not yet. He had to go to a senior judges meeting this morning. Anything that I can do for you?"

"No, I only wanted to pass on some personal information to him."

"About anybody I know?"

"I'm sorry?"

"It really is a meeting, and with more than one judge."

"Excuse me?"

"You don't have any cases scheduled with us, he's not hearing motions, you're in the middle of a trial and you want to see my judge. I can't help but wonder why."

"How many years have you been doing this job?"

"Nobody likes a wise ass. My years are mine. With this judge-ten years. With other judges, none of your business. Gossip travels fast and I suspect that you wanted to give the same advice that all his friends have been stopping in to give him. I'll tell him you stopped by if you want me to tell him. I would have a different reason for stopping if you want me to have him call you back. Just a suggestion. Maybe just buy him a drink and let him bring it up."

"What's the general consensus on the advice?"

"That he is acting like a genuine mid life crisis male who should know better. Especially with her."

"Sounds like you aren't a fan of hers."

"I don't know many of our friends that are a fan of hers. We've been in this court too many years not to be able to identify the climbers. She is definitely one."

"I don't know whether or not to have you tell him I stopped."

"I'll tell him. He likes you. Most of our court people do. You treat the staff people as though they were as important as the judges. People in support positions don't like to feel like attorneys are looking down on them."

"Katy, people like you run the show. Without support staff, the system wouldn't work. Tell him I stopped. I have to get upstairs for my trial."

"I'll bet. Some real Goombas up there with you, I heard from the minute clerk."

"So loooooong, Katy."

I got to the courtroom and was greeted by the usual trio and now they had with them Joe Storio and Lou Candido.

"Good morning, Counselor."

"Gentlemen."

"We brought the character witnesses in case you get a chance to present your case."

"Thank you."

We went into the courtroom. The prosecution team were huddled together at Counsel table and they stopped talking abruptly when I entered.

Jim came over to me.

"Lou, we're probably going to wrap this morning. We're trying to figure when we are all going to close to the court and whether you were going to present any testimony or your client."

"What do you think you would do to him if I put him on the stand?"

"I think Marilyn would have fun cross examining him. He's no Boy Scout, you know."

Jim and I had gone to law school together. He was a disarming guy who was easy going but always on top of his cases. He knew all the moves and did them all without drama but with great effect. Marilyn was not as subtle and not as astute but she wasn't anybody's fool either.

"I have two character witnesses, or should I say, characters for witnesses."

"I saw the crowd outside when we came into the courtroom. I recognized the one good looking guy. He's from one of the eastern suburbs and works for the county. I think he is also some elected position out in Penn Hills or Monroeville, am I right?"

"You're pretty good, Jimmy. I think he is a councilman and a committee man in Penn Hills. The other guy is a constable from Bloomfield. I don't have much else unless I created some reasonable doubt in the judge's mind."

"With the eyewitness testimony of three police officers from different forces, an eyewitness to the shooting by a guy that all the judges know, and the evidence that was found on him, in his home and in his car, they expect you to get a not guilty?"

"Wouldn't you?"

Jimmy laughed and then got back to it, "May I suppose that we will close this afternoon or tomorrow?"

"Figure tomorrow. Then we have the weekend to let the judge decide his guilt. Or even his innocence. I said that as a courtesy to you, Lou. I can't imagine any more than one of the counts not being found guilty for some unknown reason."

We went back in the courtroom. The defendant was unusually calm. Almost cocky. The prosecution ended the case with a summary witness who had been the detective on the gun charge. No victim, nor any known injuries. It would allow me to argue against a mandatory five year sentence if found guilty as there was no evidence of a crime being committed with a weapon, merely a discharge. The judge inquired if we were ready to proceed. We then put on the character witnesses to testify to the good character of the defendant.

On cross examination, the prosecutors then introduced all the incidents involving Mr. Mirage. His record going back to juvenile events then progressively committing more serious crimes. The character witnesses knew nothing about these or any of the reputed felons that they had in photographs alongside Mr. Mirage, together in various places. Most notably, Tigano's, the Eastwood Inn and the Holiday House. The character witnesses, of course, did not know of any of the gentlemen seen with Mr. Mirage. Finally, after what seemed like an eternity, "No further questions, your Honor."

"Any rebuttal, Mr. DiAngelo?"

"No, your Honor."

"I didn't think so. We'll hear closing arguments after lunch and then I'll take the case under advisement over the weekend. On Monday I'll deliver my verdict at 10:00. We have a judge's meeting at 9:00. Any questions?"

"None, your Honor."

"Well, what now, Counselor?"

"I go to lunch, review my closing statements, come back at 1:30 to address the jury and hope for the best."

"How does it look?"

"Are you kidding? He better get his toothbrush ready."

"But this judge is our guy."

"Listen, I don't care what you think or you think you know, he's going. Now, let me go do what I have to do."

I then left and went back to the office, looked over my notes and the proceeded back toward the courthouse. I popped in on Janet at the Carlton.

"Do you think I could get something to eat and get across the street by 1:30?"

"Sure, but table ten is taken. You don't mind sitting somewhere else, do you?"

"Not as long as I can get out in time and food is better than it was last time."

"We'll send out for pizza for you. Knock it off or you won't get a drink before lunch. Doug will be taking care of your table. What's your pleasure for lunch?"

"Jean Louis at the Watergate but he's gone. I'll have the crab cakes, please."

"I'll get everything started. How's your case going?"

"How did you know?"

"Do you know how many people come in here? It's no secret that you're involved in a weird case. One of the judges told me and was asking if you had been in for lunch."

I was seated, fed and shown the door in thirty minutes. The crab cakes were delicious as ever. More appetizing than what was coming next.

I ambled over to the courthouse, the judge came out and I made my closing argument. The judge agreed with my position on the five year mandatory as no crime could be shown other than a discharge.

The prosecution broke their argument into two parts. The lottery and the drugs. Jimmy did the lottery, Marilyn did the drugs. We were then discharged and would return Monday.

We then all cleared the courtroom.

"Can I buy you a drink, Counselor?"

"Joe Chic, I'm impressed, cocktails being offered?"

"You really don't show any real respect, do you?"

"I always show respect, I also don't miss an opportunity to call them like I see them. Let me call my office to be sure nothing is pressing. How about we get out of town? We can go to Franco's in Harmarville. I can get on the turnpike from there and you can press on towards New Ken."

"Always thinking, aren't you? OK. Shall I meet you?"

"Wait until I call the office."

I called in. Melissa had calls from Tony, Allana and the new accident case. None pressing.

"It's a deal. See you at Franco's in Harmarville."

I left and went to the office to wrap up then to the car and off to Franco's. The traffic was brutal at the construction area but opened up after the road opened to two lanes.

"Hey. Early for dinner, aren't you?"

"It's cocktail hour. I may be back for dinner later." I ordered a Macallan and passed the time of day with Maureen and Lori until Joe Chic showed.

"Let's move from the bar to a table, do they mind?"

"Not at all."

We moved to a small table by the back door exit.

"You did ok, Counselor. I know it wasn't much of a case to make but I saw what you tried. You didn't like him much, did you?"

"Not really. He wants to be important but I don't think he packs the goods."

"You can say all that you want, but he never gave up who was with him to the court or even to you. He stood up enough, what do you think we run into in our line of work? Guys with Phi Beta Captain diplomas?"

"It's Phi Beta Kappa and they get a pin after being selected to that exclusive club."

"You one of them?"

"No, but why is it you wanted to meet with me? Not to discuss my academic prowess, I'm sure."

"Did you ever get a whiskey introduced into the state?"

"Not whiskey but a few years back I was asked to have a wine that was made in New York put on the market in Pennsylvania. Pretty certain it was made by priests or in a monastery by monks. It wasn't too difficult back then. If I recall, and I'm fairly certain, I had Pio wine going to handle it. You have to demonstrate that it is a quality product and that there will be a demand for it. Somebody had to market it. That's where Pio came in. They were very gracious about it and they were to get paid for their efforts. The man who brought the product to me came through John Pisano and the guy worked for Allegheny County in some mid-level position. I think John knew him through the Sons of Italy. I remember we went to D.C. for a meeting at the

Mayflower Hotel because John was working in D.C. at the time. We all came home with a case of wine. The guy then backed out after he saw that he wasn't going to get a big enough piece and that Pio was entitled to their end. After all this B.S. he was giving us about helping the poor monks. Is that what you're asking?"

"You ain't getting' no free wine or whiskey, but we might need you to get us approval with the LCB to sell the stuff in Pennsylvania. Maybe nationally, as well."

"Each state is different. I can only do Pennsylvania as an attorney. I'm sure I can find people to help in other states if necessary."

"After I talk with my people, I'll get back to you. By the way, what's the tariff going to be?"

"Depends. Between twenty to fifty thousand."

"What? You guys are unbelievable."

"Try to get it done cheaper. It's a lot of contact work and travel to Harrisburg. You might have to make campaign contributions or go the your favorite elected state people for help."

"You let us take care of that when the time comes. I'll get back to you with the details. We'll see what it looks like."

"What about Mirage?"

"What about him?"

"You know the judge is going to find him guilty and he's going away."

"You let me worry about the verdict."

"Okay. I won't even remind you about the rest of the fee."

"You'll have it Monday. Or maybe even tomorrow night."

"Don't tell me. You know about the dinner, too?"

"You think we don't know things that go on? You're the big man tomorrow. For now. Screw up once and see how many dinners they throw in you honor. More like a going away party."

"You might consider one for Mr. Mirage while you're talking about it."

"Good night, Counselor."

As he left, I wondered how secretive these guys were since everybody seemed to know about the dinner Saturday at the club. A new whiskey product. Interesting. Whiskey from where, I wondered? Off to home, take-home from Franco's for dinner and to bed. It had been a long week. Could hardly wait until tomorrow.

CHAPTER TWELVE

Chinky and Marge, Lola and I rode together and were going to meet Leo and Carole at the club. Leo and Carole were waiting in their Cadillac outside the club at the curb. We all got out of Dean's car and exchanged hellos and proceeded down a flight of steps to the main bar area. We were met by two brothers, Steve and Gary, in tuxedos. Steve greeted us.

"Welcome to the New Bachelor's III Club. I will be providing captain's tableside service for the evening and Gary will be assisting. Will there be any others joining you?" "What is this, Steve? No, there won't be any others, but what's with the formality?"

"I'm sorry, Lou, but we got strict orders to give you and your guests the royal treatment. Especially when he gets here."

Lola chimed in, "What happened to your place?"

"Lost the lease. Property was sold. We had a month to month. Aunt Dolly's is gone."

"That's a shame. The food was great. The location, Perry Highway, was good but it stunk having to drive so far off the road over that unpaved drive. The food was worth it though."

"Thanks. Now, may I seat you?"

We were seated in front of the stage. The drink menu and food menu were presented with a flourish. We ordered drinks and a white and red wine.

"Nine o'clock and the place is empty, Steve. What's up?"

"We really opened just for you. The place never opens until eleven o'clock. It stays open until the last person leaves. I'll get your drinks and then I'll take your orders for sides and appetizers. The full menu isn't up yet, that's why we asked ahead what you wanted to eat."

Gary then appeared with scallops wrapped in bacon, and shrimp scampi.

Marge was thrilled as she loved the scampi. Chinky sits quietly and eats whatever is in front of him. Lola went to work as I did and the wine selection was a Pommard, and that was surprising as Pommards are not usually served in any place except over the top restaurants. The dinner conversation went well. Then Tony and the old man came in.

"I thought I was going to hear from you this week."

"Tony, I told you when the case was over. It isn't over yet."

"I want you to meet Raphael, my boss."

"It's a pleasure, thank you for your hospitality and the service is impeccable."

Steve's chest pumped straight out when he heard those words.

"I hear a lot about you, Mr. Attorney. I'm glad you like what we did for you tonight. I hope the ladies enjoyed it."

The ladies all gushed about everything and started to overdo it when he waved it off in a modest fashion and directed himself to me.

"Your friends?"

"This is Chuck Predmore, we call him Chinky, and his wife Marge. He's with Daily Juice."

Raphael took note without expression but his head cocked toward Chinky.

"You're with Myer and Tony Parrotta and the other guy."

"For about 20 years."

"They run a nice business. I might like to talk to you sometime about your distribution chain."

"This is Leo Parks and his wife Carole. Her father was the original PK Pecora. Uncle was…"

"I knew her uncle Jojo. Knew him well."

"Just wanted you to know who I had with me so you wouldn't be uncomfortable."

"Thank you. I have a special dessert made up for the six of you. It's a combination of cake and ice cream although it is a tiramisu and zabaglione like they used to do in the old country."

As the dessert was being brought out, suddenly people started arriving. They came straight to Raphael. It was his daughters and his nieces. We were all introduced and they all paid their respects to the old man while he sat and received them. He introduced me as "the attorney and his friends" and not mentioning any names. There was a lot of banter and casual greetings.

They left as quietly and smoothly as they had arrived. Then he rose.

"Enjoy yourselves. You should want anything, Tony will provide. Now, if you'll excuse me. I will leave you to your evening."

With that he was followed out by Tony and several gentlemen. Tony let us know that he would be right back after seeing to the safe arrival at the car waiting outside curbside.

Lola then moved closer, "Was I supposed to be impressed?"

"About what?"

"Don't be a shit. I was impressed. How did you rank an audience with his whole family?"

"Nothing major."

People started coming in and music started playing. Tony reappeared with Vinnie and several other people acting as door men and waitresses were scurrying around getting all the tables ready. They were heard to be complaining softly about not being able to arrive earlier for the set up because something special was scheduled. Leo and Carole were enjoying all the activity.

"Reminds me of when my father used to take us on vacations. Uncle Jojo and the whole family, we used to go to New Jersey and stay in the hotels along the boardwalk. This was all before gambling came to Atlantic City. Those were memories, I'll tell you."

We then drank and joked and laughed for a while longer. While we relaxed and the place filled with a large crowd, I noticed several large blonde men arrive and huddle with Tony.

Finally it was enough already. We said our goodbyes and hugged and kissed and started for the door when several men appeared behind us. They saw to it that Leo and Carole were escorted over to their car and that the four of us were deposited safely in Dean's Lincoln.

Chinky was the first to break the quiet.

"What the hell did you do for this celebration? Whatever, it must have been large, Jesus!"

Marge chimed in, "I agree. I was telling Chink when we were being introduced. What the hell was going on?"

"You both have to understand that I did a few things right. The place is open. The money is going to the right places. There's more to do yet that I haven't been asked but there were some preliminary inquiries regarding marketing product. I think it is possibly something much bigger than this club and that's why he showed an interest in your place at Daily's, Chink, because you do big time distribution. And to think it was started by three guys who got lucky."

The ride was relaxing and we were exhausted after all the hoopla and alcohol. Lola had packed a bag, and Chinky and Marge were first out as they lived between the club and my place. Lola lived a lot farther which made it easy for her to stay over. Dean could have delivered her, but hey, I was entitled to a wake up romance. I was hopeful Lola would understand as I asked rhetorically, "Shall I wake you before I cook breakfast?"

"If that means we're going to bed and straight to sleep and sex can wait until morning, yes. I'm as tired as you are."

CHAPTER THIRTEEN

I awoke fairly well rested and content. I looked over and she looked so beautiful and innocent. She was snoring slightly and, in spite of the commercials, snoring can be sexy. I kissed her ear and she made a sound of weariness although it was starting to wake her.

I kissed her forehead and she stretched. Her chest came full frontal.

"Oh my, good morning," she managed to squeeze out as she flung an arm over my chest and a leg over mine at the same time. Her lips were on mine in a slow measured motion and we began to fulfill the promises of the night before. The ritual of exploring all parts of each other was slow and deliberate and as much as any man could ever dream of having as a wake up call. The movement was rhythmic and sensuous, the various positions all worth the effort, and the slow unrushed journey to final moans and groans was, as always, an event worth remembering. We clung to each other in silence for some time and the she stretched her arms and legs.

"We will need to get going some time, won't we? It's your place but do you want me to make anything for breakfast?"

"No, I can get us whatever you want."

"I've already had what I wanted. Unless, I can move some clothes and other make-up items and so on into one of the bathrooms."

"I'll start the coffee and toast, I can make eggs any way you like or do you want cereal or something else?"

"Eggs sunny side up."

"With regular bacon, sausage or turkey bacon? Cinnamon swirl raisin toast or whole wheat?"

"My God, was I that good?"

"Better, but it would take too long for Eggs Benedict."

The eggs were done very lightly over and the breakfast was welcome as we started to become almost human after the night before.

"Tell me again about last night."

"What do you want to know?"

"I'm not going to have some one try to run me over again, am I?"

"There's no $400,000 or thirty kilos of coke waiting that I know about. This is strictly paper work for a liquor license transfer. I just happened to be able to get it done quickly and at a much lower price than one of his attorney relatives. I also did some work for him in the past that he appreciated. I get along with his right-hand man and the guy that was his second in command before he got whacked."

"Was that Sam?"

"Yes, it was. Funny, I haven't heard any rumbles going on since he got his. I would have thought the old guy and Sam's daughter would be making some noise, but then it's not my business."

"By the way, thanks for the breakfast. For the whole morning, in fact. Both hit the spot."

"I'm sure that pun was intended but I try to get to the right spot to make you happy."

"I could cook dinner for you. Every night."

"I'm going to shower and get ready for church. Father Carmine will ask about you. Did you want to come with me?"

"Sure, I like him. He always argues my case for being your regular cook. I'll clean up the dishes and everything, maybe another cup of coffee and then shower when you're finished. What flavor was the coffee?"

"Gevalia French Roast."

I showered and got dressed, came down to the first floor and saw the kitchen done to perfection. I went out to get the Sunday paper while she was getting ready. I noticed a car on the street parked with a man and a Stetson type hat on his head inside. Not unusual for cars to be on the street on weekends but not usual for people to be in them and not with a hat on their head. Kids wear those dumb caps, not dress hats.

Lola was coming down to the first floor as I returned.

"You make every dress look great."

"Thanks."

"What is the scent?"

"Romance, How about you?"

"Sanitary sewer 77."

"Come on."

"Burberry Touch."

"Were you hoping that I would touch, but, of course, I already did."

We arrived from the parking lot and the wonderful Padre was there at the front door.

"Hey, here come my favorite sinners. Good to see you don't break all the commandments and come to church. For your penance, say ten Our Fathers each and then you can go to communion because I know all your sins already, right?"

"Same old ones. Maybe a few times less. It's been a slow month for sex and work is taking up too much of our time."

"I can absolve you but only if one of you has to promise that you will make it legal one day.

"I promise, and I promise that I even tried this morning."

We settled in for the Mass after greeting Ron, Frank and Steve, the ushers. Said hello to some other friends and Sister Marlene. Father Carmine does a good job and makes his sermons interesting enough. He always ends in time for everybody to get home for the one o'clock Steelers kickoff as well. He greeted us as we left, "I got a call from that young lady in Las Vegas last week. She is doing well. Mentioned to send you her best."

"What are you, Father, his priest and his matchmaker too?"

"She really wanted to say pimp but she has more respect for you than I do."

"No, no, no. It was a young lady with a legal situation."

"How else do you think he meets them, Padre?"

"I'll see you next week. You both drive me nuts."

We left the parking lot and I suggested lunch at Bob's Garage. The idea struck pay dirt with Lola.

There were a few cars parked at the lot when we arrived. We entered and a new barmaid greeted us.

"Can I get you something?"

"Yes, a cabernet for the lady and a CC Manhattan, rocks, lots of vermouth and no cherry or cherry juice."

"Bitters?"

"Sure, why not. Where's Allana?"

A few heads turned at the question. Trona came in from the kitchen and was carrying several dishes to a table closer to the door and one for a bar patron.

"She didn't show up last Wednesday and nobody's heard from her. Why? Does she owe you money?"

"If she did or didn't, I couldn't tell you. It was a simple question. She is usually here on Sundays."

"Well, she isn't. Say hello to Melissa and Megan."

"Hi, Ladies. New here?"

"I've been here for sixteen years."

"Not on Sunday or Saturday afternoons."

"No, I'm usually evening Wednesdays and sometimes Saturdays. Megan works Sundays but has to leave early today so we're both here."

"My name is Lou DiAngelo and this is Lola."

Hellos were exchanged all around with the customers.

"Nice to meet you."

"Watch him, Melissa and Megan, he's a shyster attorney."

"Only with shyster clients."

"Will you need menus?"

"I don't think so. I'll have the Devonshire, no French fries. Lola, going for the soppresatta and cheese sandwich?"

"Great guess. Nice to see that you didn't forget me after all this conversation with other ladies."

We settled in and engaged in the usual bar talk. Sports, politics, who we saw lately, who died recently. As usual someone had a legal question to ask that they just can't hold back from asking, often to show how smart they think they are.

"Is it true that if you lose your license and have to turn it in, that your suspension doesn't run until the state gets the license? I'm trying to get my license after a three year suspension, but the state is telling me I didn't send it right away so the suspension didn't start running. Is that right?"

Lola jumped in, "He's off duty today. Here's his card, make an appointment. On the other hand, if you want a really good lawyer, I can give you a card for one of the attorneys at my office."

The customer alternately was surprised, laughed and then apologized for asking.

"You have my card. Give me a call. I'll see what we can do for you, but the statement is correct, the suspension doesn't start until the license is received in Harrisburg. There are still some steps you have yet to take. Give me a call."

"Thanks, Lou."

"Thanks for giving him my card and the clever remarks."

"It gets tiresome when people do that to you at the bar. I'm sure he wouldn't want to have to fix a drain or wire the room while he's at a bar. Especially when he is drinking a drink that you bought for him."

"I bought a round of drinks. Thirty bucks tops, if that. If he calls, which is fifty-fifty, I make a hundred times over. When I go to the Calla Lily, Lisa always says that they light up a sign outside, 'Lou's here', and the bar fills up. I buy the bar a drink and it's a hundred bucks later. You realize that I have a half a dozen cases from there totaling over thirty thousand dollars. Does that sound like a bad return?"

"Why don't you just advertise?"

"It's more fun drinking. Did you ever see some of those attorney commercials? They are so bad that I was thinking of doing one just for yuks. I'd get some of my friends and clients to stand behind me with dark glasses and say the firm name. Then say 'We make problems disappear, right, guys?' to which they all nod 'yes'."

"That would be a laugh."

"What do you say we wrap up lunch?"

Bob then came over.

"Any ideas about Allana, Lou?"

"No, Bobby, why do you ask me?"

"I thought you were her attorney."

"So that doesn't mean that I keep tabs on her."

"Just asking."

"Nobody just asks, Bob, what's on your mind?"

"Joe Chic was in a couple times a week before she didn't show. He was talking to her a couple times as well. I saw all this on my remote over the bar. I heard that you were involved in the Sally Mirage case, Joe Chic was interest in Mirage, the same attorney on all the same cases."

"What's you interest?"

"Several. She owes me a little money, but more importantly, I am wondering if I have anything to worry about."

"Is there something that you aren't telling me that gives you cause to worry?"

"None that I can think of, but you know how those guys are. They sometimes imagine problems and then the problems become real."

"If I hear of anything or get a feel for something, I'll get it right to you."

"Thanks. Megan, give them both a drink."

"I'll take a rain check, Bob, give me the chit and I'll cash it in next time. Better for you anyhow, as it guarantees my return."

"You say that like you as a customer is a plus."

"Hey, Hey."

"Just busting them. See you next time."

"What a life you lead. Always something going on and always so mysterious."

"Life is full of mysteries."

"Especially with your friends and clients."

"We all came up in an unusual way. Fortunately, most of us got out of the environment. Some of the guys got city jobs. You meet all the guys who became bar owners. Some became doctors and lawyers but other guys have a nature for wanting to outsmart the other guy. They always said that money is sweet, but money won gambling or gotten by some scam is so much sweeter."

"What do you think about Allana?"

"I don't know. I have something scheduled for her. I hope something materializes by then."

We headed for Lola's house and made a very casual goodbye.

"Thanks for the weekend, it was very nice."

"Very nice? You remind me of George Segal in *A Touch of Class*. He says to Glenda Jackson when she makes that remark 'Very nice', that's what you say to the mailman when he brings you a Christmas card. That's what you say to your relatives. But not to someone with whom you have just been locked in heavenly transport."

"Oh, my God. Well, you're not George Segal."

"And you're sure not Glenda Jackson."

"Just as good, she got an Academy Award and how do you know that I wasn't acting?"

"You can be replaced, you know."

"By Glenda Jackson? That movie is from the 70's. Good luck."

"Thank you for the nice weekend. Goodbye."

"When will you call?"

"After I find out if Glenda Jackson is busy."

"Okay. Wednesday it is."

"Call you Tuesday."

"That's very nice."

With that I headed back to my place. Bob's comments about Joe Chic wandered through my mind on the way home. Jimmy Pi had made the same type remark. There was a lot of activity and I wasn't the least bit sure if any of the dots connected.

After putting the Corvette away for the week, I went upstairs to unwind for tomorrow. I made a small pot of espresso. Lit up a Corona Padron 1926 collection with a Maduro wrapper. I clicked on the television for the news and especially to see the weather for the week, hoping that the weather prediction would have some relationship to what was really going to happen. Looked like a decent week. The Mirage trial would be over. I had several items to get off of my calendar. But Friday golf looked good. Maybe even Wednesday and Friday. Then a breaking news story. Aren't they always "breaking"? This one was, however. A body found in the trunk of a car at the airport. They were working on repairs to the short term parking when a workman noticed the license place was missing. It was parked too close to the area under construction and had to be moved. Closer investigation caused some concern and the security people called the local police. Body of a young female, stabbed forty-six times. How is it always forty-six and how do the police know the count? Unfortunately, we now knew where Allana had gone and why she didn't show up for work.

CHAPTER
FOURTEEN

The courthouse was busy as usual for the time of day. The group was stationed in front of the courtroom. They all looked like the cat that got the canary.

"Morning, Counselor, have a nice weekend?"

"Couldn't have been better."

"Ready to go to work?"

"As ready as I'll ever be."

Mirage was laying back a little from the group. He came over.

"Good morning, Mr. DiAngelo. How you doin?"

"I'm fine. How are YOU doing?"

"I'll hold up."

"No pun intended, I hope."

"Excuse me?"

"Never mind. Let's go."

We entered the courtroom. He had on a wine colored suit and matching tie with maroon patent leather shoes with maroon suede vamps. He looked the part. I wondered if he brought a toothbrush. His wife was with him. I didn't know he was married. She was a very pretty young natural blonde and seemed extremely nervous. Not what I would have expected. No heavy mascara, no bouffant hair and not even chewing gum.

"All rise. This Honorable Court is now in session."

The judge came out on the bench and greeted everybody.

"Will the Defendant approach the bench?"

We then walked up to the bar before the judge and were accompanied by the prosecutors.

The judge reviewed all the evidence and commented on the defenses, character witnesses, closing arguments and then inquired whether Mirage was satisfied with his representation.

He answered yes.

"Then, if there are no other questions or matters, I now pronounce my verdict."

The judge congratulated counsel on the presentation of both sides of the case then read off all sixteen counts and found him guilty on fourteen of them. The shooting was reduced from attempted homicide to illegal possession of firearms, as he didn't have a permit to carry. It also removed the automatic five year prison as it wasn't used in the commission of a crime. The judge then ordered a pre-sentence report and released Mirage on his present cash bond pending a date for sentencing. He still had that cocky air to his demeanor as we left the courthouse.

"I want to thank you, Mr. DiAngelo, I appreciate all you did in the courtroom."

"You're welcome." I thought he had been schooled to express his appreciation and it seemed a little out of character but he performed.

Joe Chic then came over.

"Thanks, Counselor. The balance of your money is at your office. It was delivered while you were in court. I need to talk to you in detail sometime soon. Can we meet sometime this week?"

"I'll be having dinner at the LeMont Wednesday with my lady. Did you want to meet with me at the bar before I have dinner or will this be a longer discussion?"

"It will be a very long discussion. Pick another night."

"Tomorrow look okay for you?"

"Sure. How about we meet at the bar at Franco's in Harmarville at seven thirty, then we can go to the back room for privacy?

"Ok. Let me have a number where I can reach you if anything comes up."

"You can call Rosa Simeone at the restaurant. She'll have someone get hold of me."

"See you tomorrow, Joe."

Back to the office. The pre-sentence investigation would take at least six to ten weeks before a sentencing date would be set. Mirage was out on bail until that time, at least.

Almost like clockwork, when I got back to the office the intercom buzzed.

"Rosa Simeone on the phone."

"Hello, Rosa."

"Hi, darling. Everything go all right with the case?"

"Depends on who you ask. The judge is happy, it's over. The prosecution is happy with all the counts that were found guilty. The judge congratulated me and I got paid. Maybe you ought to ask Mr. Mirage."

"What do you hear about the assault case?"

"Nothing recently, but I think that the ball was in your court as to whether your guy was worth the money to settle the claim."

"His mother is my first cousin. I would never hear the end of it if we didn't do something to help him out. We are going to get him a spot with the Pirates in the club room bar at the ball park for the rest of the season and the money will be paid from the front office to an account for his income until we will get the money back. Had to pull a few strings but sometimes favors come back."

"Then we're ok for the fourteen thousand?"

"I guess that's the best you can do?"

"I think so."

"I love you, Louie. Get it over, sweetheart."

Put a call through to Tom Eveready. He was agreeable to the fourteen thousand. I still had to get releases from Blue Cross and Blue Shield. I put Jennifer on that call to them. The deal was no recovery of medical expenses but all pain and suffering. The coverage people usually didn't put up a fuss in that situation.

"Mr. D, Detective Bruno on the phone."

I picked up, "The constabulary is up and about early today, I see."

"And a good morning to you, Counselor. Done with court today?"

"Word must travel fast."

"We had a case down the hall. Guy took a plea to manslaughter for a reduced sentence. The reason I'm calling is about your former client, Allana."

"I saw the paper. Nasty business."

"Can I see you to talk about the case?"

"Not today. I have a lot of work to catch up."

"Tomorrow sometime?"

"Be here at about ten, ok?"

"See you then."

"Mr. DiAngelo, Filo on the phone."

"Hey, Paisan, how are you?"

"Couldn't be better."

"I heard the case went as expected."

"Expected by whom?"

"Expected by all the people in the know. You had a situation that couldn't be alibied away. The guy was eyeballed by everybody and everybody that knows him knows he's trouble."

"So I am gathering."

"But that's not why I called you. I hear you are doing some liquor work for the old guy. I was calling to see if you had any more news about that property in upstate New York."

"Like what?"

"Like what was going on up there."

"I don't know that anything was going on up there."

"Because you believe all your clients, right?"

"That's not entirely true, but then I don't have to believe anything. I just go by what they tell me that doesn't go against what I find as evidence on my own."

"How about if I tell you that the guys from Hazelton and Buffalo were very happy up there? A lot of items passing through. Some from the other side of the Atlantic."

"Why would I care?"

"Because some of the items have an effect on what we are doing with our guys. You realize that JB and Joe Chic are not in step with the old man, or did they not tell you?"

"What would I care about their relationship?"

"If it affects their income when you're successful in your next outing, it means a whole bunch."

"What's the next outing?"

"Whiskey."

"What is that supposed to mean?"

"It means that an application for an import/export license for whiskey is a likely scenario. Your friend from Daily Juice was asked some questions and he mentioned it to Meyer and Tony. They smelled a rat and made a few inquiry calls. The info came back to your efforts as they need to be able to make money by cornering the market."

"I haven't been asked yet."

"You will. When it happens don't forget the property in New York. Leo didn't have any idea but his in-laws were very helpful in getting a safehouse set up for some people. That was the start. It ain't over yet. Cy will be in town tomorrow or the next day. Can we have lunch or drinks?"

"Sure. It depends on whether anything else comes up."

"I understand. By the way, how is Tony's wife holding up?"

"I haven't seen her. Why do you ask?"

"For my personal reasons. I'll call tomorrow around eleven to see what your schedule looks like."

"Talk to you then."

Back to setting up the Partition proceeding and reviewing the file but with that nagging feeling bringing me back to Filo's statements and questions. When Bruce sent the process server out, shots were fired at them. He needed to get the property secured by the Sheriff just to get the property ready for sale. The question about Tony's wife was unusual as well.

"Telephone, Mr. D. JB for you."

"Hello, Counselor."

"Good morning."

"Can we get to see you sometime soon?"

"What did you have in mind?"

"How's your schedule?"

"I can see you in my office tomorrow. I have a detective coming in at ten. How about eleven for you, then it will really be cops and robbers."

"Funny man. How about I hook up with Joe Chic and see you at Franco's tomorrow night? Will you have enough time?"

"Don't you guys ever keep a secret?"

"Not when we're all in the same boat. That all right with you?"

"Sure."

"Thanks. You know we all like you because you've always been right with us and you're not one of those stuck-up fancy lawyers that thinks he's something special."

"Thanks for the compliment but the fee doesn't come down."

"Now you're talking like those other lawyers for sure. I'll see you tomorrow."

Now the plot really thickens. The characters are coming in crowds.

Spent the next couple of hours getting the evidence on the Partition in perspective.

"Mr. D, there is a Mrs. Cuccinetti on the line."

"Good morning, Mrs. Cuccinetti, Attorney DiAngelo here, how are you?"

"I'm a-fine. I'm a-wonder if I can make a point ment to see you?"

"What's the matter?"

"I get news from a-New York about-a my other son, Anthony. I'm a-no sure what to do."

"What's the news that you got?"

"He get his truck a-stolen and call-a the police. The police come and they arrest-a him. Something about a fugitive from justice and a warrant for him in a Las Vegas. I'm a-no understand what this is all about. Why he got arrested? They a-steal his truck."

"Where in New York?"

"Indian Lake."

"OK. Let me make a few calls. Is your phone number still the same?"

"Yes-a, sir."

"I'll get back to you."

"O, God a-Bless. Thank you."

"I haven't done anything yet. Let's see what I find out. I'll let you know."

I looked up Indian Lake on the computer. It was upstate Adirondacks. I called the Sheriff's office in Hamilton County.

"Hello, Sheriff's Office, Deputy Carter, how may I help you?"

"Good morning, this is Attorney Lou DiAngelo from Pittsburgh. I'm calling at the request of my client regarding her son, Anthony Cuccinetti. I am told he is under arrest in your county."

"Let me transfer you back to lockup. They will be better able to help you."

"Hello, this is Diane, how may I help you?"

"Hi, this is Attorney Lou DiAngelo from Pittsburgh. I'm calling regarding my client's son who is thought to be in your lockup, named Anthony Cuccinetti. Can you tell me anything?"

"Sure. He was arrested on a fugitive warrant from Nevada, I think Las Vegas. It was a harassment and terroristic threats charge filed by a former employer. Let me get the docket. Hold on."

She came back and told me it was Joe Gags at the Riviera Hotel and Casino. Some two years old. I thanked her and started to call Bruce Bergman in New York but then it dawned on me that the warrant was out of Las Vegas. We used to do junkets with the Riviera years back and Joe was in charge of customer relations. I called Mike Rhodes, an attorney that we used in Las Vegas. He was in the office and I explained the situation. He got on it and would call back. I then called Attorneys Tunney and Pukalski to have them see what dates they might be available for the first day of what I hoped would only be a two-day hearing. Tunney was his usual pain in the ass evasive self. Mark, on the other hand, was up front and quite talkative. We exchanged war stories for a few minutes. I got the best dates from him and dictated a letter advising both counsel that these were the dates for the hearing and for them to be ready to proceed. Tunney would have to adjust. Good treatment for his sneak character and mealy-mouthed platitudes.

"Mr. DiAngelo, Attorney Rhodes on the phone."

"Mike, what's doing?"

"Your guy is on the street."

"What?"

"I got hold of the Riv, got Gags. He called the Magistrate and withdrew the Complaint."

"Hey, hey. Hey, that's fantastic. I owe you big time. What shall I send you?"

"If it were my client, that would have been a five thousand dollar phone call. Guys in the can and now he's out. Who's your client?"

"An Italian widow from the old neighborhood trying to help her only remaining son after the older one was murdered."

"Could you make it a little more heart rending? Did you want me to send her the five large? Tell her to light a candle for me. When you next send me a paying client, don't look for a referral."

"Thanks, Mike."

I called and broke the news to Mrs. Cuccinetti. She started to cry on the phone.

"Oh, you have to come-a to my house and I cook-a for you again. Just like-a before. When you going to let me try to be-a nice-a to you like-a you nice-a to me?"

"Let me call you next week, okay? We'll arrange something."

"That-a be nice. Oh, God Bless, when-a my boy be home?"

"I don't know where he's going, but if you have a number for him, call and ask. I'll give you the Sheriff's number and maybe they can tell him to call his mother."

"Thank you, thank you, Madre mia, thank you."

Now that I got all my merit badges for the day, I started to look for what I needed to do to pay the rent.

"Mr. DiAngelo, Judge Pasquarelli on the phone."

"Your Honor, how is his eminence?"

"As you say, couldn't be better. I called to see what you are doing these days. I hear you stopped in the other day, but I don't see you at the Carlton like before or at Costanzo's."

"What are you doing at Costanzo's? That's a hike for you for lunch."

"I stop for cocktails. Sometimes dinner. Sometimes both."

"Dining alone?"

"Not you too? Does everyone have to peek over my shoulder?"

"I didn't do anything other than ask if you needed company."

"I guess you're right. Maybe I'm getting a little paranoid. I wouldn't mind having a drink with you. You could tell me how the legal profession is getting along."

"Maybe later this week."

"A deal. Give me a call. I'll see what my schedule allows."

Now, a chance to unwind.

"Hello, where have you been?"

"Do I have the right number?"

"I'm not sure. How do you know I'm not taken and on my honeymoon?"

"I figured I would have known since I was friendly enough to get an invitation."

"How about to an execution?"

"Ouch! It hasn't been that long."

"It seems like it. How about I walk to your office and we have dinner or you do Steak Diane?"

"I've worked hard enough today. Do you need to freshen up or straight from here to dinner?"

"I could use the shower in your office and I always have a cocktail dress in case of emergency. We could then go to Bravo Franco's and then home."

"I'll wait for you at my office. Let me know when you start down here."

Now I had my dinner schedule for two days along with a cocktail hour and a home-cooked meal in the near future. The Partition case was scheduled, Anthony Cuccinetti was out of jail, the Mirage case was over and he would be taking Anthony Cuccinetti's place in population. Things were looking good which had me scared because when all looks like sunshine and roses you always get the feeling something not so good is going to happen.

"Mr. DiAngelo, a Mr. Cuccinetti on the phone. He said that you would know what it was about."

"Hello."

"Mr. DiAngelo, I'm Anthony Cuccinetti. My mother told me that she called you and I am out of jail. I wanted to thank you."

"You were lucky. We happened to get all the right breaks and if it had been done in a real professional manner, it would have been a big fee. My friend that pulled it off isn't sure how much longer he wants to be my friend if it keeps costing him money."

"Mr. DiAngelo, I will be coming to Pittsburgh next week. Maybe when you have a chance, maybe next week, we can talk.

I'm not a bust out but I couldn't post my own bond and my mother wouldn't know how. I will be willing to pay your friend whatever and I might have something for you that may be of value in addition to paying whatever you think you should be paid. You know my mother told me all about how you helped with that episode with my brother and her at the time."

I thought to myself this son seemed to have more going for him than his brother, Louie Cooch, and somehow still seemed to have a little thief in his blood. Oh well, from the Avenue, everybody recognized a little larceny in the heart of everyone else.

"Mr. Cuccinetti, that…"

"Call me Anthony or Tony, not Mister. May I call you Lou?"

"Sure. I'll tell you what, next week we'll have dinner at your mother's. Will you be able to discuss whatever it is at that time?"

"I think so. I'll call you when I get to town. We can then decide what day is good for you."

"It's a deal."

What now, I wondered. Someone wants to pay money after the case is over and offers to pay what is asked. On top of that, a home-cooked meal, I'm sure, with all the trimmings.

My cell phone rang.

"Hello."

"I'm on my way down. Are you ready to get ready?"

"See you when you get here."

I started to wrap up. It felt good that I had gotten a lot of work off of my desk. Now for a pleasurable evening with my woman of many pleasures.

The late part of the staff were still in the office. The staff that arrived early had departed for the day when Lola appeared in the waiting room. Jennifer buzzed her through the door. They greeted each other like old friends. What better way to insure your position than to make friends with the staff of your significant other. They could always be on the lookout for your benefit if they liked you. They all liked Lola, which was a mixed blessing for me. Any hint of competition and their loyalty would be tested.

"Hello, handsome," and she slipped her hand into mine and kissed me politely. A nice demonstration to the staff that her man was spoken for and for them not to get any ideas.

"Hello, gorgeous. Your shower awaits."

She proceeded through my office to the facilities with a large purse and a silk garment bag. I think I bought her the purse at Saks. I heard the shower and started to get ideas but remembered this was my office and my staff was still here.

I went back to the Partition file to insure all was in order and looked up some legal issues. I then remembered that I had to send a letter to Mr. Mirage advising him of his rights regarding appeal and possible sentences according to the guidelines. If I don't send the letter, he may be able to argue ineffective assistance of counsel. Not that I thought anything could overturn the verdict as everything came in properly and procedurally correct, but I still had to go through all the motions. I then dictated a release for the settlement for the Simeone kid so the time spent was rewarding. It always feels good to get work completed.

My reward opened the bathroom door.

"Did I ever tell you what a lucky guy I am having found you?" She came out and the steam with the smell of perfume was absolutely intoxicating. Soft flesh that smelled good and looked good in a simple black dress. The legs to kill for and her hair was pulled back on one side and loose on the other.

"What do you carry in that purse?"

"All the necessary items to protect my appearance for a week at a time. Approve?"

"You know I do. I must be hungry because my mouth is starting to water."

"Your couch could be multipurpose, you know."

"Let's get out of here. This is a business office."

"I was suggesting business. Monkey business."

I took her arm firmly as I was getting firm and marched her out to the front door. We then proceeded to walk across Market Square over to Bravo Franco. F. Murray Abraham was to perform in a Mozart Tribute by reciting the monumental work. The streets were packed with the crowds lining up to see him and hear the Pittsburgh Symphony now sadly performing without the incomparable genius of Marvin Hamlisch due to his untimely death but with the debut of Manfred Honeck, an accomplished conductor. We made our way through the crowds to the restaurant.

Carole greeted us, "Oh my God, how good to see you two. Where and how have you been?"

"Fine, Carole. Thank you."

"Couldn't be better."

"Did you call ahead?"

"No, I didn't. Quite frankly, I forgot as we were moving around a little today. Will there be a problem getting her something to eat?"

"Her, no. You, maybe."

"I guess I'm outnumbered."

"Luig, will you excuse me a moment?"

"Sure." I watched as she went outside for a cigarette. She had been without for the last hour or so.

"How have you been, sweetie?"

"As always. Business ok?"

"Doing well. I do miss Marvin though."

"I know. Why don't you put his chair solo in the window where he sat and drape it in black in honor of him. He used to be in that seat regularly enough."

"Might scare people away. Could think something's wrong. But maybe we'll think of something."

Lola returned.

"And how has this lug been treating you, darling?"

"Almost as good as some of my other dates."

"You know what? I've been so busy enjoying myself with Carole that I haven't even thought to order a drink. Not like some other persons that drive one to drink."

"Now, now, you two, let's be civil."

"Does that mean foreplay is required or does that mean that it is optional?"

"Does it mean that it is with you?"

"It means that both of you are going to have a drink and dinner and be nice to each other."

Carole's son, Mark, then took our drink order and the other Mark, the waiter, came over to seat us. I ordered a Franciscan Cabernet and finished my Manhattan.

"Truce?"

"At least a cease fire for now. I haven't heard from you and was beginning to wonder. I've seen the staff that you have. No wonder the workmen want to know who does the hiring."

"You know I only have eyes for you."

"Yes, but a dick for the world."

"My, my, such language."

"Listen to you."

"May I apologize and remind you that all the trial work, the hearing I have coming up, the people that you met at dinner, all cut into the time that I treasure most, the time with you."

"You are lucky that I love you or that line would have ruined my appetite and probably caused me to heave lunch, which I did not have, looking forward to this dinner. Shall we, quote, be civil?"

"Civil? For now. After dinner, how about we get criminal?"

"What criminal actions. Between consenting adults and with willing partners of opposite sexes?"

"The way we will do it may be against the law."

"Promises, promises."

"Are you and the lady ready to order?"

"Saved by the bell. Yes, I think so."

The rest of the night went smoothly. Only one bottle of wine, appetizers and we split a helping of the mostaccioli with the peppers in oil and garlic.

"You two ate like you were hungry."

"She always eats well. It's a sin she gains no weight but out-eats two guys."

"You didn't do so bad either."

"The sight of her makes my mouth water and my appetite becomes insatiable."

"Dear God! Where do you come up with these lines? Keep it up though and I might stop hating you for being such an inconsiderate creep."

"Well, that's a start."

"Shall we have coffee here or at your place? I was thinking of your place."

"How many dresses do you carry in that bag? My place it is."

We headed back to the garage and she took my hand.

"I do miss you, you know."

"Don't feel like the Lone Ranger. All the actions of these cases is nice and profitable but it wouldn't be worth a damn if it didn't allow me to entertain you in the manner to which you are too fast becoming too well accustomed."

"Does that mean that you think I am spoiled?"

"Rotten."

"Whose fault is that?"

"I hope, only mine. And when we are finished with coffee I guess you will want me to spoil you again by showing my undying love and lust for you."

"Only if I can reciprocate."

"I suppose this means that we are getting along and friendly again."

"We'll soon find out, won't we?"

The drive home suddenly seemed longer than I remembered as she reached across the seat and under the steering wheel.

"Will we have time for espresso? Something looks like you are almost ready to spoil me."

"Take it easy. I really would like some espresso first. We have all night, you know."

We went in through the garage. When we got into the game room downstairs, she took my arm and effectively turned me around, kissed me with a hard wet one and then put her head on my chest.

"I really do love you, you know."

"I know and you know how I feel about you as well. It's just that our lives somehow become so hectic. I truly am sorry that I have been so busy and neglectful."

"Maybe I am just being selfish."

"So long as it means you want more of me, I accept."

I made a small pot of espresso as I didn't want to drink it all night and we had other important things that were on our agenda.

The espresso went down especially well with Molinari Sambuca as a sweetener and a pony glass of Strega. We then dispersed with the small talk regarding work and time together and proceeded to the main bedroom. Amazing how she can get undressed so quickly yet it usually takes a lot longer to get the same clothing on that wonderful body.

"God you smell good."

"That means your nose is in the wrong place, but anyhow it's Yves St. Laurent Pour L'Homme."

She slid her tongue down my chest and stomach and began making sounds that could only inspire any man with a bit of manhood about him. I took my cues and began to return the favor as she moaned in ecstasy. Then we went full frontal and managed to get our faces front to each other. The rhythm of the two bodies enjoying each other never lasts nearly long enough and after what seemed like too short an effort and not enough screams of pleasure from her, I couldn't restrain any longer. I rolled over as all men do and we gently kissed some more.

"I do love you, you know."

"You said that already tonight and you know as well that you are the only woman that means anything to me. I don't know how I could get along without you."

"You mean that? You know, you are really saying some corny lines."

"Why would I lie now? I already got what I wanted and why a man would lie to a woman."

She laughed softly and kissed me as if for dear life. I started to doze with her head on my shoulder and then we put on the bare essentials and settled for a well-deserved night's sleep.

CHAPTER FIFTEEN

I awoke about 6:30am and started downstairs.

"You want me to do anything?"

"Just stay beautiful. What's your pleasure for breakfast?"

"I'll just have some yogurt or cereal. What do you have?"

"I've got yogurt and Wheaties or Cheerios. I am going to have some turkey bacon and eggs with toast. I'll be making coffee, as well. What would you like me to do?"

"How about repeat last night?"

"Really."

"I'll get in the shower and help myself to the Cheerios when I get down there."

We finished up breakfast, were dressed and off to town for another day in dreamland.

I dropped her at the front of her office and parked at my garage, crossed over to the office where the staff was already putting out documents and showing a flurry of effort.

Tuesday's are usually slow days unless I have a motion to present. I try never to schedule motions for Monday so that I can get caught up with emails and mail from the week before.

I went to work on several files to get them in order for anticipated action. Before I knew it, the intercom brought me to attention. "A lady on the phone, says she's the daughter of your client."

"Hello, this is Attorney DiAngelo," I said as I picked up the phone.

"Mr. DiAngelo, this is Sam's daughter, Joanna."

"Good morning. How may I help you?"

"You knew my father for a long time, didn't you?"

"Yes, ma'am, I did. I'm sorry about your loss you understand."

"Thank you, you're very kind. My father told me that if I ever needed any legal advice to not go anywhere else but to your office. He said you were standup and could be trusted."

"Thank you, I appreciate that I had his confidence and trust, I don't know how this relates to this call, but I am sure that I am going to find out in a minute, right?"

"Very good. You know my husband as well, right?"

"You know that I do."

"Has he been to see you recently?"

"I would rather not answer that question, if you don't mind, and I might like you to not insist on an answer because if I answered, it might be a breach of confidentiality."

"My father was right about you, I guess. Let me ask this, can you handle my father's estate and help me get all his affairs resolved?"

"Certainly."

"When can I come in to see you?"

"How about Thursday? I am going to try to get together with some friends tomorrow and today is pretty much booked."

"What time?"

"How about ten? This way the traffic should be gone."

"You're on Fourth Avenue, near Market Square?"

"You got it."

"What should I bring?"

"Everything that you have with regard to your father. Also, give me a phone number where I can reach you if anything comes up."

I was wondering what this meeting could be all about, as it didn't seem as though the estate was the most important thing on her mind. I'm sure her father had most of his assets hidden anyway so what could there be to probate?

"Mr. DiAngelo."

"Yes?"

"Three detectives here to see you."

"I'll be right out." I straightened my tie, smoothed back my hair and tucked some papers out of view. "Well, good morning, gentlemen. You brought the whole force. Come on in. Did she offer you coffee, water of whatever?"

"We've been pulling extra duty so we asked for three coffees."

"I'll add that to my consultation fee for you guys."

"Thanks, counselor. You met Detective Villalpando last time, remember?"

"I do."

"This is Detective O'Leary. He's new to homicide from burglary so we are taking him around for a couple of days. You don't mid, do you?"

"As long as he doesn't read me my rights."

"Thank you for taking the time to meet with us. You remember we wanted to talk to you about Allana."

"I do remember."

"Can you tell us anything about her? She's dead so the attorney-client privilege doesn't count anymore, is that right?"

"Pretty much. I'm not sure that I know enough about her to help you, though. What do you think I can tell you that you probably don't already know?"

"She was married to Danny Deacon, has children by him, he was trying to get partial custody and wasn't paying any real support. Does that ring a bell, Counselor?"

"Good work. You guys know as much as I do."

"There are some things not in your file on Allana. We are aware that you represent some people. We didn't file a protest to the license as you know."

"Thank you. I did know and my folks are grateful."

Detective O'Leary chimed in, "Does that mean no murders in the near future?"

"Easy, partner, let me ask the attorney the questions. There is a lot of action in town right now. Am I telling you anything you don't know?"

"No. I noticed a lot of names also."

"And Sam was whacked a little while ago. There was no follow up to that. Seem a little strange to you?"

"As a matter of fact, I had the same thought."

"As an attorney, we realize that you aren't allowed to keep quiet if you are aware of a crime about to be committed or being planned."

"Where did you go to law school? That's pretty good."

"Come on, Mr. DiAngelo, we've all been around a long time. We don't have any real leads on the killer of either Sam or Allana. Somehow, however, I think there is a relation."

"Well. Let me see if I can help you. She's not Sam's girl so that wasn't the reason for her death. Sam wasn't cheating on her so she didn't kill him. What do we have? A lot of faces, maybe to decide if Sam's death should go unanswered. A bar maid who gets to see a lot of people and some of them may be a part of the discussion."

"That's where we were heading, too."

"I don't have any real clues as to who or what. She didn't say anything to me."

"Do you have any ideas on Sam's case?"

"You know I really don't. That's one I can't figure out. His son-in-law called me about the killing the night that it happened, and I went to the viewing and saw a lot of people but nothing unusual. I had no idea of anything that he did that deserved a killing. He was always a reliable and standup guy. He served his boss well, didn't do drugs, not much of a gambler, drank socially, and had a girlfriend but that didn't add up to a bullet in the brain. Nothing that I could guess."

"How about an import/export license?"

"What about it?"

"I hear that it's in the making."

"I think you're right, but how would that amount to a killing?"

"Bingo."

"You really think so? You guys have a tape or something?"

"Without snitches and tapes, I don't know how we would solve the tough cases. The stupid perps on the other ninety percent is one thing, but anybody with any sense can cause trouble to an overworked, understaffed bureau."

"I'm not volunteering to pay more taxes but I do agree you guys are short staffed. And most of you are good guys, without mentioning any names of your former partner, O'Malley."

Detective Villalpando spoke up, "Anything that you can tell us about that import/export?"

"Hey, Detective Villalpando does ask questions. Not really. There's nothing that I know yet. As soon as I am ready to file an application, since it's public record, I can let you know."

"Thanks, Counselor, and we thank you for the coffee. Was that Brand X?"

"We brew it especially for when police show up. Besides, it's usually been cooking since six o'clock this morning. You're lucky, this was fresh."

"Next time you visit one of your clients at the lockup, we'll return the favor."

"Okay, get your Boy Scout troop out of here. I have paying clients coming in."

Just then the door opened and JB started through the door.

Detective Bruno turned around toward me and over his shoulder smiled and cracked wise, "Make sure you get your money upfront." He then looked and JB and directed his crack to him, "Don't drink the coffee, he makes it especially bad for cops and crooks."

JB looked a little confused but not overly amazed. He shrugged. "I knew his dad when his father was a beat cop and then became a vice detective. Nice people you have at your office."

"That's funny, he was saying the same about you. Come on in. Would you like some fresh coffee?"

"As a matter of fact, I would."

"Jennifer, coffee please. Make a fresh pot."

We sat down and the conference began.

"So, what are the fuzz looking for?"

"A murderer. Who killed Sam and who stabbed a bar maid from Bob's Garage."

"Yeah, I heard about her. A shame. The police thought they had it bad with organized crime. They didn't know how bad it would be with disorganized crime. We all had rules then. We knew what the police could allow and what the public wouldn't. We tried never to cross that line."

"What can I do for you, J?"

"That import thing the old man was asking about. Is it going to be a problem?"

"Not that I can see as of yet. I haven't been officially asked to do anything yet."

"I see, I see. Can I retain you?"

"Sure. It depends on what you want me to do and so long as I don't have a conflict of interest with other clients."

Somehow, in my mind I smelled a little race to get something done.

"I want you to look into the export license and tell me what has to be done to get one of them licenses."

"It's called an import export license. You can send and receive."

"That's good, that's good. OK, that's what I want you to find out for me. How much will you need?"

"My usual retainer is $5,000 but make it $500 for just giving you an overall picture. If I need to do more, I'll let you know.

At that time, I will want the $5,000. Do you have a corporation set up yet?"

"No."

"If you really want the import export, you will be best served incorporating. All that for a later day. Start thinking about a name for the company anyhow."

"Thank you, Counselor. Here." He handed over five one hundred dollar bills. And we parted.

I was working on cleaning up some files and getting cases in order when the phone buzzed, "Filo on the phone."

"Hello, Filo."

"Cump, how are you and how's lunch look?""

"I forgot about lunch, but it is fine. Let's see what time it is, 11:30. Tell you what, I'll meet you at Ruth's Chris in thirty minutes. I'll call over and get us a corner table so you can feel free to speak as you might want."

"Deal. See you there."

I started wrapping up, called over and they had us in and at a table in the back. I started to wonder what else was going on. This was a morning to end the week, not the beginning.

Weather was nice enough walking across the PPG Square over to the restaurant. Looked like golf would be on the agenda tomorrow.

"Mr. DiAngelo, good afternoon."

"Hello, Kirsten, and how are you?"

"Couldn't be better as I've been told. Your lunch partners are seated already. I'll have a Manhattan over to your table directly."

I was led over to the table and I hope that I didn't show that I was surprised to see Zartan and Billy seated with Filo. No Michael this time.

"Gentlemen, good afternoon."

"Hello, Counselor, you know these gentlemen."

"Indeed, I do. Good to see all of you."

"Can we get something?"

"It will be on the table shortly, thank you for asking."

"Getting a lot of visitors lately, aren't you?"

"Now just what is that supposed to mean?"

"Hey, don't get upset, just a comment. And maybe if you're nice, I'll tell you why you're so popular. Billy and Zartan have an idea that you are going to get some work setting up an import export license. Billy came in from Wilkes-Barre to have a meeting with some local people here and they told him that you were being mentioned as the attorney. Your friend Chinky's name came up as well. He's the guy with Daily Juice, right?"

"Yes, that's right."

"Well, Zartan has a few friends that were looking into the same thing. You also have a friend that owns a house in upstate New York. The house was occupied for a while but no longer."

"The local police and my attorney friend had an idea that it might have been a meth lab."

"What do you know about the house in New York?"

"Nothing really. When the Sheriff or the private process server went out to serve the papers the people in the house took a couple shots at them."

The faces around the table exchanged knowing glances and disbelief but apparently were aware of something related to the occupants.

"Did the process server or Sheriff ever make service on the people that were there?"

"As a matter of fact, I don't think that they did. I think my friend in New York had to get an Order of Court to allow the property to be posted for service."

More knowing glances exchanged, this time favorable.

"Is the property still there?"

"As far as I know. I am pretty sure that it is up for sale. Do you want to tell me what this is all about?"

"Sure, just a couple more questions. You have a sentencing hearing coming up soon on Sally Mirage, correct?"

"This is also correct. Do I win the prize now?"

My drink arrived and I sipped after a salud to all present.

"Do you think Sally is going to jail?"

"Yes, and for some length of time."

"Ok, Counselor, here it is. Zartan and Billy may have an interest in securing a motel along either the Parkway West or East. East may be along Ardmore Boulevard or West out by the old airport. Either way, I suggested that they use you to do the transfer with the LCB. What will you need for a hotel license?"

"Probably five to ten thousand and costs of filing and license charges. The license might be worth up to a hundred thousand, you know. Have you approached anybody to find out what they want?"

"Zartan has an in with the people that own the corporation."

"Why not make it a stock purchase deal instead and then all we need are people who will pass the BCI background check and have a manager that will also pass."

"How about if I am manager?"

"Sounds like a deal to me. The paperwork for the hotel transfer is a little more work so it will probably be closer to the ten thousand."

"Not a deal breaker."

"Why all the other questions?"

"That was for a different reason. Hope you didn't mind."

"It was all a matter of record."

"Now we can eat. All this questioning got me hungry. I can see why you attorneys can get tired. It takes up a lot of energy asking all these damned questions."

Lunch went well. Conversation mostly about old timers like Joe S. from Hazelton, DeLouise from over near Scranton and a host of other names with funny stories attached to them. like going hunting with one guy who fired his shotgun right next to his leg because he wanted to make sure that it was loaded. I thought as crazy as the shooter may have been, how crazy must you be to go shooting with him having a loaded weapon in his hands.

I noticed Cy was a lot quieter than usual and Zartan was not saying anything. Not unusual for him, however. Most of the chatter came from Filo, as was his custom.

"Gentlemen, I have to get back to work. Thanks for lunch."

"One last thing, Luigi, we will be calling next week probably about the transfer. Let us know when we call if it looks like there is any problem."

"Look forward to it."

"Be careful with your other goombahs out there. Some guys are more solid than others, you know, and some are not nearly as standup as the people at this table."

"I'll talk to you next week."

The walk back to the office didn't have as much sunshine. I didn't know if it was because of the company I had just left or if it was actually a change in the weather.

Back at the office and going through the mail. Notice of the date for sentencing for Mirage had been set. The application of the Greek for his pardon application was scheduled the same day. Amazing how often cases get scheduled the same days. Fortunately, the sentencing was in the afternoon and the Pardon Board hearing was in the morning. I was scheduled to be third up on the Pardon Board calendar. No telling when the sentencing would be heard depending on what other cases the judge had going that day or the day before.

I then dictated the appropriate letters to both clients advising of the dates and where/when to meet me. and reviewed the partition hearing, which was coming up soon enough.

I had a preliminary hearing scheduled for the next day on a DUI out in East Pittsburgh scheduled for 8:30 A.M. Called the client to be sure that he would be there.

Next I reviewed a bankruptcy request from Marty Lazzaro. He had a civil case he was trying to settle after he had been appointed as Special Counsel for his client. There was also a worker's compensation case pending for the husband of the Plaintiff.

I reviewed the bankruptcy of Marty's client and saw that we could file a motion that would allow settlement and distribution. No claim was allowed by the creditors for pain and suffering payments so the proceeds were safe from creditors. I/we/he could try to conclude the worker's comp claim of the husband.

I reviewed three motions scheduled for Bankruptcy tomorrow afternoon.

Jennifer buzzed me, "Mr. DiAngelo, Lola on the line. Can you pick up 125?"

"Sure, thank you." I picked up the phone. "Hello, gorgeous."

"We're on for tomorrow night?"

"We are."

"At the LeMont?"

"Yes, darling."

"Will you be driving or straight from town?"

"Hold on, I'll pick you up at your house about seven thirty and then we move to dinner."

"What's on for tonight?"

"I have a meeting at Franco's in Harmarville with a couple of male clients."

"Make sure you don't get too friendly with the waitresses or any of the female customers."

"O ye of little faith."

"Oh no, I have a lot of faith in your ability to attract trouble."

"How else do you think that I stay in business?"

"I'll count the minutes until tomorrow."

I packed my briefcase with the file for the next day's prelim and headed for the door.

Franco's was fairly busy according to their lot and the construction near the Hulton Bridge caused a traffic nightmare. Fortunately, the restaurant was on the opposite side of the lane closure.

Maureen, the hostess, was seating people when I came in and Peter and Maureen, the waitress, came up quickly to cut me off at the bar.

"You might want to have a drink at the bar first. Seems like there is a slight disagreement among your friends."

"Among means more than two. If there were two you might suggest that the argument is between my friends. How many people are waiting for me?"

"There are four guys back there."

Lori came over, not her usual smiling face. More like a concerned or a serious look, "Manhattan or Macallan?"

"Macallan, please. I might need it, I suppose."

"They got a little loud back there. Peter tried to calm them down. They then realized that they could be heard and were in a public place. They were talking about territory. I'm sure they will need you to do whatever it is they pay you to do."

I nursed a few sips to have my palate whetted and then took a healthy swallow.

"It's show time, folks!"

I turned and proceeded to the back. Joe Chic, JZ, Tony and Raphael, the old man was moving about from his home base. No longer with his right hand man, Sam, either.

We all exchanged hello's and I sat at the opposite end from the four who sat at the other end and across from each other.

They all mumbled greetings. The old man spoke up first.

"Everything going all right with you, Counselor?"

"Couldn't be better, thank you."

"I hope we are not inconveniencing you by having this meeting."

"It's no inconvenience. I was asked to meet here by Joe Chic and JB suggested he was going to be here as well when I spoke to him, but I didn't know it was going to be a convention. Not that I mind, but I am not sure what I am supposed to be ready to do for all of you."

Sly grins from JB and Raphael. No emotion from either Tony or Joe Chic. It appeared that all was not happy with the family of friends.

"If we want to import whiskey, we need an import license, right?"

"Correct. From Alcohol Tobacco and Firearms. What they call in West Virginia, revenuers. I think they might be the successors to the publicity hound, Elliot Ness."

"What do they investigate?"

"The applicant, the type of import. You might have to deal with customs as well."

"How tough do you think it will be?"

"Depends on who is sending you the product and who is applying for the license."

"They do a background check and then interview and what do they do with the supplier?"

"Depends on where it originates. Can't trade with Cuba, for instance. Probably not Iran either."

All heads turned to each other.

Joe Chic spoke up, "I asked you to meet me here before anybody else was involved to find out how soon you can get started."

"I can get started as soon as you tell me who the person will be signing the application. If you want to do it individually or as an LLC or corporation. Most young lawyers like LLC. I like corporations. It makes you do required things that keep you on top of the program."

"I like corporations, too. I'll call you this week or next and provide a name. I may even have an old company that we could use."

"Have to be careful there as there may be old taxes. If taxes are current, no problem."

"I'll call you next week."

"Is that my cue to say goodnight?"

"Thank you for coming. We may have to decide some things where you don't need to get involved. If you want a dinner or to have another drink, let us pay for it. I'm sure the time you spent tonight will show up on the bill in addition."

"Right again. Good night, gentlemen. Thanks for the offer but I'll pass. I have an early case tomorrow."

I left as I didn't want to continue being available since the meeting didn't need me anymore and I didn't want to be dragged into the middle of anything.

CHAPTER SIXTEEN

I dragged myself out of bed. I had poached eggs and turkey bacon on the side with toast and coffee from Gevalia. It was an African blend. Got everything in order, showered and started to drive over to District Justice Scott Schricker in Turtle Creek. for the DUI prelim scheduled for eight thirty. I was going in the opposite direction from the rush hour traffic. The waiting room was filled to capacity. The police arrived from East Pittsburgh and my client was there as well. If I got out of here quickly and if my motions in Bankruptcy receive orders by default, I might be able to get a golf game in with Leo, Kent and Greg.

The arresting officer came over.

"You Attorney DiAngelo?"

"I am."

"What are we going to do today?"

"I was reading over the papers and probably need to find out if there is anything more you were going to add for the probable cause to stop the vehicle."

"I don't think so. He was over the line a couple of times and didn't come to a complete stop at the stop sign. We pulled him over and we smelled a strong odor of alcohol."

"Alcohol doesn't have a smell, officer. If that's the basis I might ask you to identify the brand, the type, and whether you are able to tell the difference between beer and whiskey or vodka or rum. All that aside, this is his first arrest, no?"

"I think so."

"No accident or anybody injured?"

"No one got hurt."

"Probably I can get all of us out of here so long as you don't have a problem with ARD. He didn't give you any trouble, did he?"

"No, he was very cooperative, but he couldn't pass the field sobriety tests and we couldn't let him continue to drive. If anything were to happen after that we might be responsible."

"You don't have any trouble with ARD, do you?"

"We won't, no. It's up to the Court. We're just the arresting officers."

"Let me see what I can do. That's the right approach, officer, for both of us, just doing what we get paid to do."

I talked to my client and it was his first arrest. He was afraid that he would lose his job but understood that if he wanted to pursue a not guilty, it would be much more expensive, time consuming and chances of a win were not favorable. After I explained and he said he understood all the license suspensions and that he wouldn't have a record after expungement, he agreed to waive to court. The officers were as happy as I was that we could leave early. The magistrate was also a good guy who had his head screwed on the right way and moved us up on the list to get us out. A triple play, the court, the officers and the attorney just doing their jobs.

I called from the parking lot to the office. All three cases had orders entered disposing of the motions. The motions were all pro forma and no major impact on the other side. Two were ended by stipulation and one defaulted.

The usual suspects were all agreeable to play. I called Dave at the pro shop and he had no events and we were all right to tee off after lunch. I sent a text to all confirming the lunch and tee off as well as Dan Merchant, the General manager at Hillcrest Country Club, so that we would be sure to be expected.

Lunch, cocktails, golf, back to the clubhouse for wrap-up thirst quenchers and the day was ending nicely. Or so I thought.

"Lou, have you heard anything from the U.S. Attorney in New York, what's his name, you know."

"Attorney Robinson.

"Why?"

"I was just wondering. I know he said I wouldn't have to appear but, you know, I just wanted to be sure everything was all right."

"You worried about something, Leo?"

"Well, you know, Carole Ray's got a family and sometimes they get worried if everything's not right. Especially if there is a federal attorney looking in on the situation."

"I haven't heard anything from New York. You can tell everybody that we have nothing to report."

"I'm sorry, Lou, but you know how they think."

"Is there anything that I should know that you aren't telling me?"

"No. Nothing like that, just being as careful as I can."

My cell phone rang.

"How did your golf game go?"

"Great. Nobody slowing us down, nobody was behind us and in a hurry. We got around in less than four hours. We had the usual drinks and laughs."

"What did you shoot?"

"The score card says more or less eighty four. Kent has a seventy-six, Greg had an eighty-five and Leo admitted to an eighty-two. We all played fairly well. Not too many mulligans."

"Are we still on?"

"Certainly. I am heading for the shower and should be at your place at seven thirty as promised."

"Love you."

"Love you, too."

"I don't believe you said that. Oh my God!"

I ended the call and Leo took my arm.

"I hope you aren't mad at me. I had to ask, that's all."

"Did somebody put the arm on you to inquire?"

"Not like that, no. Just a passing reference that was a friendly question."

"Now you have me wondering who and why anyone would ask. You're not holding back anything, are you?"

"Lou, I don't have anything to hold back. We bought the place and rented it and you got us out of it. That's all there was to it."

I made my way to the locker, showered and on to Lola's. Traffic was a nightmare but I was in no hurry. I wondered about the questions with Leo and decided I might call the U.S. Attorney tomorrow. As an attorney, it wouldn't be unusual to be following up and insuring all was well.

I rang the doorbell and she answered the door in her birthday suit.

"Am I early?"

"When the man I love says the love words to me I want to let him know that I am immediately ready to show my appreciation. In fact, we don't even have to go to dinner."

"You will disappoint the folks at the LeMont."

"I won't disappoint you," she said as she closed the door and ate my face and inspected the insides of my mouth with her tongue. She then slid down to start to undress me while making friends with the best part of my body. Talk about helpless. She then led me to the bedroom. I had stopped resisting, if I had even begun to resist, and we were at the bed.

"Why are you covering up now? You were naked at the door."

"A little modesty is supposed to make you want to strip and take complete advantage of me."

She must have been right as I did want to take advantage of her and the entire situation. How horrible of me. I was going to continue finding where and what caused her to react with the thrust of a race car and allow her to demonstrate her intense love for me while only having to struggle to make sure that this episode didn't end too quickly. We managed to stay on the bed while moving to various and equally comfortable positions until finally I couldn't hold back the inevitable. Thank God for women having multiples. I always figured that a five to one ratio was a good exchange for the actions of two nubile people in heavenly transport.

She held on with a serious grip and seemed entirely satisfied. I wonder how a guy could fake orgasm. That's a tough one but thank the powers that be, she wouldn't need me to try to pretend that she was special.

"Tell me."

"Tell you what?"

"What every woman wants to hear."

"You don't have to cook tonight?"

"Tell me again."

"You don't have to cook tonight."

"Tell me what you said on the phone, that you love me."

"What I said on the phone, that you…"

Her elbow was perfect into my ribs.

"OK, OK, I love you, I love you."

"Was that so hard?"

"Not so hard as some things that aren't so hard now. It was funnier, though, you must admit."

We snuggled for a short while and my stomach started to present signs of lack of attention.

"It's getting on to nine o'clock and no dinner. I better call the LeMont and apologize for not showing."

"You don't have to call, I talked to Dana and told her we wouldn't be able to make it."

"What?"

"Yes. She wanted to be sure everything was all right. I told her that I wanted to have you for dinner. She laughed and understood. I took the liberty of having Alexander's make up some tripe for dinner as they only do it as a special. I figured you would deserve something special in addition to what you already had that was special. Of course, Alex and Jimmy sent along salad and a side of eggplant. All that and I have the wine. You could eat and be home by bedtime."

"Well, aren't you something."

"Tell me you love me more often and you might never know what you'll get for a special."

"Wow, you are getting me a little afraid."

"Of what? Enjoying the best things in life? Wasn't it your friend Dan McFadden that used to say, there's nothing bad you can say about sex?"

"I would add that some sex is better that others, but none is bad."

"Where is he now?"

"Northern California somewhere. He was some government official but I never ask about his source of income. He got married, I think, to a gorgeous attorney as well. She flew in with him to a class reunion."

"Male or female?"

"Him? As straight as they come, no pun intended."

"Speaking of come… come hither and let's eat. You know I can't eat tripe."

"A lot of people can't, I am blessed, I can."

The rest of the evening went along well. I even was allowed to leave without doing the dishes. A great day. Golf, got four cases on the right track, got my lady to cook after she cleaned my jodhpurs and then send me home happy. I had a few appointments tomorrow, but nothing pressing. It seemed like everything was in order in my world.

Arrived home, finished coffee in the pot from the morning, watched the last few minutes of the local news and to bed. Enough for one day.

CHAPTER SEVENTEEN

The traffic was lighter than usual and the trip to the office uneventful, at least for me. There were the usual accidents on Route 28 at Harmarville or RIDC Park, on 79 near Bridgeville, and a disabled vehicle on the Parkway West at Greentree. The usual over height truck trying to go through the tunnels wasn't present today as reported by Kathy Bergrin over KDKA radio, and the weather would be agreeable enough that we might even see the sun.

I parked the car and walked? jogged? strolled? over to the office.

I went over the mail and started to review the papers for both the argument for Mirage and for the parole board for the Greek but was interrupted by the intercom. .

"Mr. DiAngelo, Judge Pasquarelli on line two."

"Good morning, your Honor."

"Morning, Counselor. How's your day look?"

"I have a couple appointments, no court, but I have a dinner appointment with a widow who has two sons that I had as clients."

"How old were the sons? Or, better yet, how old is the widow?"

"From the old country and the old neighborhood. The sons are my age."

"Just keeping you honest. Can you get together for a drink sometime?"

"I could probably do a late cocktail with you. She is from the old school so dinner should be over by seven. Does that work for you?"

"I have a jury starting today so I will probably be on the bench all day and have some office matters to clear up after that. I can meet you around seven, I would guess."

"Where shall we meet?"

"No place too public. I wouldn't want anyone to think judges are friendly with attorneys."

"How about either Alexander's in Bloomfield or Cioppino's in the strip?"

"I can afford Alexander's, you can afford Cioppino's."

"The drinks are on me at Cioppino's."

"See you there. I have some questions I think you can answer."

"See you then."

I went back to the preparation for the two matters and my intercom told me that my ten o'clock had arrived.

"Good morning, Joanne, please come in and sit wherever you feel comfortable."

"How about on your face?"

"Excuse me?"

"I need to talk to you and don't need you to soft soap me."

"Would you care for something to drink? Water, coffee, cyanide or are we in a better humor than your last response?"

"I need you to help me and not try to be a diplomat. I know that you know all the dirty secrets about my husband and my father. Because of your position, I asked for this meeting. You have been acting on behalf of both of them for years. They trusted you and you did all the dirty work they asked you to do. I need help and I don't need you trying to fuck around and try to charm me."

"I was merely being polite. Which I might say is more that you are doing at present. How about we level off a little and I ask my usual initial question. How may I help you?"

"I need to know how this license deal is going and what my father left for me that I can claim, and not through my husband."

"I have you here as my client and I will give you the best advice that I can without compromising any confidentiality restrictions. I am sure that I can do that in most of what you may ask but we might go into areas where I may have to restrain or decline to answer. We won't know until we really get into the issues you want to discuss. Let's give it a try."

"My husband tells me that I am going to be the name on the license. Is that right?"

"That is right."

"Why me?"

"Because you are as pure as new fallen snow. No record, no criminal activity, a married woman who has an interest in a business that is legal."

"Will I have any authority with the license?"

"It will basically be yours. Your name is on the license, you are the owner. They may run the business but they can't do anything without your approval."

"Good. Now, what do you know about my father's girlfriend?"

"I take the fifth. That isn't a legal question so I will hope that you appreciate that I choose not to get into gossip or any incidents that don't require legal expertise."

"What about Tony's adventure?"

"I'm not sure I know what you are asking…"

"What is he doing with the old man and all these people that can't speak English?"

"If I knew I probably wouldn't be allowed to answer, but I truthfully have no idea what you are suggesting."

"All these blonde, blue-eyed guys and girls that keep coming to pick him up. Is he running some sort of escort service or does he have some sort of illegal immigration action?"

"I have no idea. I couldn't answer if I were doing anything as counsel but I am not. Now to estate matters."

"What shall we do about my father's stuff then?"

"I don't think there is much that you have to do. The property is owned by your father and mother. It will go to her without any legal proceeding. I am assuming that there were no deed transfers from both of them such as a trust or transfer to you in addition to them."

"I don't know and my mother never asked. Can you find out?"

"I can have my staff go online or check the records at the Recorder's."

"What about cars and bank accounts?"

"Car will have to be transferred with the Pennsylvania Motor Vehicle Bureau and bank accounts signed over. Do you have any idea of any bank accounts?"

"I found some statements in his desk."

"What we'll probably do is open an estate to all of these transfers take place. I have an associate, Rod, that I will have meet with you to set this up. He can have it done without much fanfare and not expensive either."

"Does Tony have to be involved?"

"That's a funny question, but the answer is no. He has no standing here. You know what, it dawns on me that your father had a will. I'll get it from the archives and see what it says. I can assure you, though, your mother gets everything as it was a standard will, each spouse leaving everything to the other."

"Thank you. How long will all of this take?"

"From start to finish, about nine months. It will be mostly paperwork and then a court decree making it all final. We might have some inheritance tax on the transfers but that won't be much."

She then began discussing all the good time and vacations with her dad. She seemed a little upset that nothing had been done since her father's death. Since it was obviously not a natural death and Sam had been a higher-up in the ranks it did seem a little out of character that no subsequent bodies hit the pavement. She went into various aspects of the liquor license and I told her that I would probably use Charlie and Lou Caputo to handle the transfer with me to insure no delays or problems with the LCB. I had worked with their grandfather years before and they succeeded to the practice after I left and their father passed on. She seemed to remember all the same memories as well of the grandfather. He handled a different group than the one Sam and Tony were working.

"How much will the liquor transfer cost?"

"To you, nothing. To them, fifteen to twenty thousand."

"Good, I'm worth it. Do I get to get paid?"

"You'll have to talk to Tony and the old man about that?"

She then left. She looked pretty good, as wives and daughters of serious people go. She dressed conservatively not like in the movies with exaggerated makeup and hairdos. You could almost mistake her for a schoolteacher. She also seemed worldly wise as well, a great asset in this case. She also piqued my curiosity about all the blonde, blue-eyed people. They certainly weren't Sicilian or Calabrese.

"Mr. D, a Tony on the line. Says you will know."

"Thank you."

How quick I get a follow-up call. Was he sitting outside in his car?

"Hello, Tony."

"Good morning, Counselor. Is my wife still there?"

"She just left. You just missed her."

"Too bad. Anyway, it looks like the import export deal is a go. Do you want to get started on and what do you need?"

"I need names. People involved, corporate name, stuff like that."

"Do they have to have no history?"

"It's not like the LCB but it will be something you don't want to be a problem."

"Joe Chic is clean and so am I. Can we do?"

"You had some arrests but as I recall no convictions, am I right?"

"You walked me out of federal court, don't you remember?"

"I do remember. That was the motorcycle gang case. There was an undercover agent that became part of the gang, but you were lucky enough to not be present when any crimes occurred. We walked out. Unusual to walk out with your client after a prelim in federal court. Then I had to lend you money to get home."

"That's right. And I still haven't paid you back. At any rate, that is how we want to try to make it a go."

"I'll probably have Charlie Caputo and Lou Caputo help out on this one as my staff is overworked now and I like having backup in case any hearing or license app review is needed and if I have any schedule conflicts."

"Just so it doesn't double the tariff."

"It won't."

"Good, let's get it going. And I will want to see your friend Chinky again as well."

"I'll see what I can do."

"Let me know what his schedule looks like and we can try to accommodate. Maybe another dinner out at the club."

"I'll call him and see what he thinks. I'll try to let you know this week."

"Thanks, Counselor."

I started to get the Partition hearing file put in order and answering correspondence.

"Lola on your line, Mr. DiAngelo."

"Good morning."

"It's almost afternoon, can I buy you lunch?"

I glanced at the desk clock. It was almost noon.

"Sure. Can you afford the Carlton?"

"I can't afford not to. The finest place near the courthouse with the best service."

"Hey, has Kevin been working on you?"

"It's got the ambience, the wait staff, the food and it even has cloth napkins and cloth towels in the restrooms. All the important stuff."

"Sweet Jesus, you sound like a commercial."

"I'm sick and tired of peanut butter sandwiches in the office."

"I'll call Janet and tell her we're coming."

"I already did. She has table ten open and waiting. See you there in fifteen minutes."

I closed up all the open files and headed uptown. It was all uphill so I worked up a slight bead of perspiration and was primed to quench my thirst.

"Mr. DiAngelo. Good to see you."

"Always my pleasure, Kevin."

"My sister tells me she saw you at dinner up at the Calla Lily Café."

"She and Harve were having dinner. I think Harve had just finished golfing with Don, the golf pro consultant from Dick's. I had to hear all about Harve's good golf round."

"I also hear you are doing work for the some union people."

"Excuse me?"

"Remember my cousin Jack Shea is the President of the Allegheny County Labor Council. He gets to talk to all his people and they tell him about what he has to know to be aware regarding all the labor people. As a result, any union people that are in town and should be acknowledged are brought to his attention."

"Well, he isn't coming up here to spend union money for lunch. He has to eat in the cafeteria with his people. Besides, this is the other end of town for him as well. What did he have to say, now that you brought it up?"

"He tells me that you are in with some high steppers. These are guys that get involved with a lot of high risk enterprises."

"Like the restaurant business isn't the toughest racket in the world anyhow."

"That union has had some rough times. I also need to be up on who my competition might be if they decide to open anything in downtown."

"You're in luck, they're not coming to town."

"I wouldn't want to lose any of my best customers like you."

"You won't."

"Your lady has a job, doesn't she?"

"Yes, why?"

"Because that union does a lot of favors for other labor people. Jack tells me that girlfriends of some leadership guys in the teamsters and ironworkers have their mistresses working in unionized restaurants and hotels. All that goes through Rose Simeone and her husband and Joe Chic. The point being, if your lady needs a spot and you went to Rose then you might feel an obligation to frequent their place and I would lose the little bit of spare change that you allow us to enjoy here at my place."

"You knew all this without Jack telling you, I'm sure."

"Lou, everybody sees what goes on and you know that all restaurant people talk to one another. They see some very attractive lady that can't count to ten consistently getting plum work assignments and schedules and they aren't happy about it. They also are happy then to talk to the U.S. Attorney that we hear is showing an interest in the activity of that union. All this so I don't lose you as a customer."

"I don't know, the food might be better in Allenwood or Danbury. My friends tell me if you are going to get pinched, make it to Washington or Westmoreland County where the food is downright edible."

"You show no mercy."

"Hi, handsome."

"Hello, gorgeous."

"Miss Lola. Thank you for gracing my place."

"Hello, Kevin. I thought I better take him to lunch or I might never get a call."

"And a welcome sight you are. Maybe I should buy you a drink."

"Hold on, Kevin, don't break your no hitter at this late date. Or is it only for women that you buy drinks? Forget I even suggested even women get one on the house. Janet, may we proceed to table ten?"

"It's ready and waiting for you. Miss Lola called and I knew we had to be nice to her at least. Dave Tomer will be your server today."

"Thank you."

"What's the occasion?"

"I did need to get a lunch break from sandwiches and it gives me a chance to see you as I recall you are booked most nights this week."

"I might be able to double or triple out tonight and I may be able to arrange a dinner after a meeting this weekend out at the club in New Ken again."

"That was an interesting evening. How are you doubling out?"

"I have Mrs. Cuccinetti tonight and the Judge Pasquarelli after that. That should free me up a little."

"Is he bringing his girlfriend?"

"You know about that?"

"Remember me? The girl you love works for attorneys, too."

"They said something?"

"Oh, Lou, for God's sake, don't you think people see the obvious.? She's been after him for so long. He even moved out from his wife. I'm sure it's not so they can discuss cases."

"Well, she was a looker when she was younger. Still attractive and has all the right equipment."

"Yeah, but he gives her respectability in the judicial world. He's been around a long time and is well respected. Or at least, was."

"In answer to your question, she will not be there. Let's have lunch."

Michael arrived with my Manhattan and her cabernet. We toasted and looked at the menu. Michael then went into action. Bill stopped over to say hello as his manager duties required.

"Special today, as if you didn't know, is tilapia. Shall I tell you how it is prepared?"

"I'll have the southwestern salad, chicken and dressing on the side."

"I'll have the original salad with the original dressing and the grouper."

Lunch went well and Lola did, in fact, pick up the check."

"I'll let you know where, when and how. Probably call you tomorrow, ok?"

"Works for me. Love you."

"Talk to you tomorrow."

Back to the office and called Attorneys Tunney and Pukalski. I gave them the date for the hearing. Tunney started to whine about how he might need a different date because of a conflict and I told him in no uncertain terms to be at my office at nine thirty that morning. If he didn't arrive, the hearing would proceed without him. If he had a problem, he could petition the court to try to accommodate him.

The rest of the afternoon was mostly housekeeping. Soon enough, it was time to head over to Larimer Avenue and Stoebner for Mrs. Cuccinetti.

CHAPTER
EIGHTEEN

The traffic was unusually light and I got over to Larimer while it was still daylight. All the old places were gone. Tony's Barber Shop, Mayflower Drug Store, all the bakery shops. At one time, there were eight different Italian bread makers. Now, only Stagno is still in the area. The Meadow Grill structure is gone as is the Red Eagle Club, successor to the Genovese Restaurant. A lot of the big names used to stop for dinner while in town performing. Wayne Newton, when he was very young, Nick Adams, and a host of others. Of course, all of the important mob guys if they needed to be in Pittsburgh. Now only cousin Mike's Auto Body. His place even expanded as a training facility for educating youth on auto repair and servicing. His lot was very close to Stoebner as I turned up the alley. Where once parking spaces were at a premium, there were only two cars. One in front of Mrs. Cuccinetti's and one much further up the alley. I parked behind the car in front of her place. It looked like a rental. It probably was and it probably was for her son. I remembered that he was to be in town this week.

I knocked on the door.

"Hey, Mister DiAngelo, come stai?"

"Bene, bene. And how are you, Mrs. Cuccinetti?"

"I'm a-fine, joosta fine. I'm a-really happy, I have-a you come over and a-my son he's a-be here with me also. It's a good a-feeling to have a-my son, Anthony, and also for you that I get to cook. Let me take-a you coat."

"Thank you."

A tall, slender man appearing to be in his mid forties to fifties entered the living room form the back of the house. He was nicely dressed and didn't look any worse for wear after spending a little time with the constabulary in the lockup.

He came over directly to me with some enthusiasm.

"Mr. DiAngelo, you know how good it is to thank you in person and to meet you. I really appreciate what you did for me."

"You give me entirely too much credit. It was really Mike Rhodes. And we were both lucky. I'm not sure I know how we managed to get it done that quickly. Usually you get to spend enough time just being processed. I can assure you it was a lucky set of circumstances."

"Call it anything you want, but it was great to breathe free air again. Also, great to be able to meet you at my mother's house."

"Your mother is a great lady."

"She told me how you helped her after my brother died. Thanks again."

"Ok, let's cut it out now. You're going to embarrass me."

"That's a-nice-a you two boys get to know each other, but you have-a time after you munge. Come in-a the kitch and we sit and have a little antipasto before-a dinner."

We went into the kitchen table and she had the same fancy glasses that I remembered from the last time and the same wonderful soppresatta and olives and cheeses. The wine still tasted home made. Anthony was eating more that his slender build would have you expect.

"You like-a gnocchi?"

"That depends."

"On whether it's-a made with ricotta or potato, is that-a whatta you think?"

"Exactly."

"I'm-a never make with a potato. Madre Mia, Always with-a ricotta."

"Salud!"

The gnocchi were as light as a feather. She had field greens and asparagus with a melted cheese over the top. I ate as much as I could but the dishes never seemed to get empty. The wine was as light as any home made wine could have been. She then brought out the napoleons from Stagno's. I was embarrassed that I had forgotten to bring dessert.

"I am so sorry, please forgive my rudeness, I forgot to bring dessert."

"You brought the napoleon last-a time you was-a here. My boy, he rode up to Auburn Street and got them at-a Stagno's. Some-a people like the Moio's , some like-a Stagno's. Stagno's is closer."

"That was a lovely meal. I can't thank you enough."

"I'm-a thank you. You get-a my boy back-a home to me."

Anthony then leaned over and exchanged some small talk as his mother poured some espresso. He asked if I remembered the people that used to live on Stoebner, Jiggs and Mary, Anthony Imbarlina, the Dapper family, Rose Belvedere, Nino and on and on. Most of them I remembered. We sat as he lit up an unfiltered Camel and then he surprised me.

"You are representing a Mr. Mirage, aren't you?"

"Yes, I am. Why do you ask and how does that come up?"

"While I was in lockup, I had several guys pass through my cell on their way to court or to be processed. Guys talk while they are in the clink. One of the passers through mentioned that there was a big move under way that he had heard. He was hoping to get out so he could get in line to maybe make a score. He heard that there were a couple of guys that were in the can that knew about it as well. They were not American and they could screw things up. Mirage was going to meet them in the can for info or something that was needed. He was going to be sure that they were okay, I think he said. He thought that I was something big as everybody knew that my warrant came out of a Las Vegas casino. It made me look like I was somebody important. I think he also mentioned that people from outside of the U.S. were making some moves as well."

"How did you tie me in with Mirage?"

"He mentioned that they had this lawyer from Pittsburgh that used to do work for the Vegas casinos and he was named after some angel. I figured out the DiAngelo from what my mother had told me and he confirmed my lucky guess."

"I'll be."

"Funny how some things come together."

"Is there anything else you can tell me?"

"Not that I recall, but if I do, can I give you a call?"

"Of course, you can call anytime. Remember, I'm friends with your mother."

The talk turned around to his plans and what he intended to do in the future and the night ended. I made my way out from their house with all the kissing and hugging as is the custom and began the drive back to town. Cocktails with Judge Pasquarelli at Cioppino's.

Traffic was unusually heavy in the opposite direction. Some event going on or late night workers. The bar was almost full with the up and comers. Probably the new breed working the rounds to try to make a mark in their chosen profession. The judge was at the far end with a tall drink.

"Luigi, I started a tab in your name. Christian said that it was all right. He never knew you to walk a check."

"Never by mistake anyhow. Sometimes I let the bar know if I was unhappy."

"Not tonight. I couldn't take any more bad gossip. It might even make headlines."

"Who would want to read about a has-been judge?"

"Ouch. A has-been already?"

"Better than a never-was, no?"

"Remember, I am the same age as you."

"Maybe younger."

"Maybe."

"My scotch may be older than you."

"That's funny and you know it's not true, but all the b.s. aside, how are you really?"

"I couldn't be better, you know that. You're the one everyone is concerned about, I hear."

"Can't a guy enjoy his life a little? Why is everybody so concerned?"

"You want me to really tell you?"

"Sure. That's one of the reasons why I have a drink with you, because I know I get it straight from you."

"For starters, everybody, well almost everybody, that I know likes you. You've always been an upright guy. In the district, then when you moved up, Orphan's Court, all the other benches where you sat. You were always a straight shooter. Then you got hooked up with her. She's not what you are. Between you and me, I know her a lot longer than you do or will. She's always been a good looker, but she has always been making a maneuver one way or another to help her move up the ladder. You aren't the first and you won't be the last. You had a stable marriage, good family, now this. It's not the fairytale ending that everybody thinks happens. You got a whiff of what she's selling and you lost your pathfinder. In spite of it all, everybody still likes you and we'll all be there when she finds a new path. What will you do? Is that plain enough?"

"Why don't you tell me how you really feel? You wouldn't hold anything back, would you?"

"You mean about what she puts up her nose?"

"I know about that."

"You don't share, I hope."

"That's a little more for the young crowd. No, I just find her amazing. I can't seem to get enough of her being around me."

"I guess your kids have some animosity."

"Of course. They love their mother and are trying to not hate me."

"I'll bet they hate this one enough, though."

"They try to stay distant from it. They say they just want both of their parents to be happy. It's not like they're children. They're both adults. We do okay, considering."

"Can we drink now or do you want more up to the minute gossip?"

"That's enough. I needed to get a relaxing drink and I knew I could count on you."

"Let me have the Macallan. Is it 1864 replica?"

"Close enough. Neat, correct?"

"Neat it is."

"How's your life going, Lou? Tell me something good."

"You don't want to talk cases, do you, I hope. You know I usually stay away from judges and lawyers when I drink as they always 'have an interesting case'. If I wanted to hear about cases, I'd rent a DVD, enough about cases. My lady is doing well. I have a trip booked to the Bahamas, may make it to DC soon. Make the rounds, The Prime Rib, I Ricci, Teatro and Goldoni, if it's still open. Try to find out where Roberto Donat is now. That's how you blow off steam."

"That plain enough all right. You may find out someday that in spite of all the precautions you take, sometimes something happens ad you get swept away. I can't begin to explain but it was a life changing experience. I was overwhelmed."

"So, the devil really does wear Prada? Believe me, I understand. Every guy should have his heart broken seriously once in his life. It's a feeling that you will never forget. He should also get swept away once in his life so that he knows both sides."

"Are you speaking from experience?"

"Certainly. I was very young when my heart was broken but it was my fault. After I screwed up the romance, she wouldn't even speak to me. I was nuts. Looking for her, trying to run into her. She wound up marrying a guy I knew. That turned into a disaster and I got over her but I never forgot the lesson it taught me. Then, years later, I met another someone. She was beyond belief. I was planning to marry her and had all kinds of wild ideas, just like you are now. Thought that she was the crème de la crème. I was called over by a couple of friends. They were very firm in their advice. They told me to back off. When I was still ready to make a move, she moved in with some other guy. I was amazed, but not like the first heartbreak because I put my heart on alert. No headlongs again. No open heart surgery ever again. I tell you this because I don't want to see you in that position. If you've never had your heart broken, then I don't feel sorry for you. If you have and you didn't learn anything then I still don't feel sorry for you. If you have had your heart broken and you think she is the crème de la crème, you're on your own, big boy. You're not a kid anymore and you're on the ride for all it can bring. Like my friends warned me, I am warning you. She's poison. Protect yourself at all times especially in the clinches. I had a friend, he met a beautiful woman. I represented her as well. She was no a bad lady, neither was his wife. This woman was beautiful. He was experiencing what you are experiencing now. Everything that romance stories tell you love is all about. Sex, gentleness, caring. Easy to do when you don't have to deal with all the everyday bullshit problems that he and his wife had to handle. No children problems, no work problems, just euphoria. It's worse than meth or crack. That little fur ball can get a guy to do crazy things. Even to and from judges. Get it?

"You're probably right about the feeling because that's how I do feel."

"You're only human in spite of everyone kissing your ass when you put on the robe and strut into the court. She, on the other hand, is evil."

"You really don't like her."

"It's not a question of like. It's just what she is. A frog is a frog and a scorpion is a scorpion. You know the story, if the scorpion stings the frog swimming across the lake they both die. Frog from sting, scorpion from drowning. Couldn't change their nature, they both went down. Myself, well none of your friends, want to see you go down."

"Okay, enough already. I, at least, know now what my friends think. All the same as you?"

"Some hate her for real, but they all love you for real as well."

"So what's going on with your practice and love life?"

"The usual daily cases and love life is as good as I could want it."

"You still seeing that secretary from that law firm?"

"Yes… she deserves better."

"Why do you say that?"

"She would like a permanent setup. I got out of one marriage and am still treading water."

"It's all right to be cautious. Once burned, twice cautious, you know. I hear you've got some interesting people in the courthouse. A few well-known names were there the other day. What can you tell me?"

"Some punk kid got in a scrape. I'm not sure why all the big names are so interested in him. One of the other guys I know made some insinuation that I wasn't supposed to win the case. That they wanted the guy to go away. I can't figure out why, but they will get their wish. He doesn't think so but I keep telling him he better pack his toothbrush. His wardrobe will be state provided for quite a while. I also have a Partition case where I am the master. I have Tunney on the case."

"That weasel, is he still practicing?"

"It looks like it."

We continued our small talk for awhile and had a couple of drinks and then called it a day. I could sense that he was feeling more upbeat than when he arrived. It can be a tough life being a judge. Most people don't realize it but for a decent attorney, it's a cut in pay most times, a thankless spot and you live in an isolated world for the most part. We said our goodbyes and I headed for home. The thought of what Mrs. Cuccinetti's son had told me kept me awake thinking for awhile but my body needed all the rejuvenation that a good night's sleep could bring.

CHAPTER NINETEEN

I had nothing scheduled that I could recall and decided I would check the calendar after I arrived at the office. The parking lot had the FULL sign flashing. It had been raining heavily so the Mon Wharf Parking Lot was probably closed. I wondered what genius designed the parkway to run along the river so that the road and parking would be closed when it flooded regularly.

I was reviewing the partition hearing exhibits in my office when the intercom buzzed.

"Mr. DiAngelo, it's U.S. Attorney Robinson on the phone."

"Thanks, Tiffany."

"Mr. Robinson. Good morning."

"Good morning, Attorney DiAngelo. Thanks for taking the call. I needed to see if you could shed some light on a situation that we uncovered in the house in upstate New York."

"If I can."

"We found some traces of meth behind some furniture. We also found, which is more disturbing, some fragments of U.S. Passports. They were in the outdoor fireplace."

"What does that suggest to you?"

"A lot of possibilities. I wonder if you could inquire of your client to see if there is any information that he might be able to provide? If we need to, I might have to have him appear."

"Let me see what I can do."

"You realize that there is a lot of family in his life. She has family and he has a history as well."

"I understand but I am sure that he had no involvement in any of the activities that you just described."

"But he may know who did."

"I'll get what I can and get back to you. If it looks like he did anything wrong, for sure I'll want to talk to you to see that he is protected as much as possible. Both from you and the other guys."

"Thank you."

I called Leo, but he wasn't available so I left a message that it was important. I went to the items on my desk and started on the import export app.

"Mr. DiAngelo, Mr. Filo on the phone."

"Thanks, Sherry."

"Hey, Paisan, what's up?"

"The motel deal is a go. How soon can you get started?"

"As soon as you tell me which one, who will be the officers, are you buying stock or real estate, or both, who will be the manager and a million other things, but most importantly, when you get twenty thousand dollars in my account."

"Form a corporation, call it OCIVRES, the owners will be me, Zartan and Michael. They get equal shares. It will be a stock transfer. Each of them get twenty four and one-half percent, I get fifty one percent. It will be the one located by the old airport."

"Nothing for Billy?"

"You want heat from the feds? So, far as you know he has nothing to do with the deal. I'll have the info faxed over to you. Give me your fax number before we hang up. How long will this take?"

"I once did a transfer for Costanzo's in forty-five minutes. This may take at least that many days. Since it is a stock transfer, the only impediment will be the LCB investigating the officers holding the stock. You had your record expunged, Zartan is clean, what about Michael?"

"He's clean."

"Should fly."

"How are your other clients doing?"

"All my clients are doing well."

"You know who I mean."

"You know even though you are all my friends, or at least most of you are, I can't tell you anything about them which may reflect on their cases."

"Watch out for those guys who are the friendliest."

"Give me the fax number and we get moving."

Back to the other license and the partition case.

"Mr. DiAngelo, Mr. Parks on the phone."

"Thanks for getting back to me."

"Hey, when your attorney calls, you have to get back to them. What can I do for you? Better yet, what are you doing for me?"

"I'm keeping you on the street. And maybe keeping you from being under the street."

"What does that mean?"

"The U.S. Attorney from New York called. They found some traces of meth and pieces of passports. He wants to know if you know anything about that."

"You know that I don't. I never saw the place."

"So you know who rented the place?"

"The rental agent would know."

"Do you have a name?"

"It was Carole Rae's cousin. I think JoJo's sister's kid. Let me call you back. I'll get the number from her. She's at work right now."

"I'll be waiting."

I hung up and went back to preparing the partition papers. I called Lou and Charlie Caputo. I got voicemail and on both of their extensions. I called Charlie on his cell phone and got him directly. He was in court in Greensburg. I filled him in on the transfer and that I might need him for backup as I had my staff working overtime. He was agreeable as always and was able to talk more than I expected since he was in Judge Caruso's ante room awaiting his turn to negotiate his case.

"Mr. DiAngelo, a Tony on the line. "

"Thank you."

"Good morning, Tony. How can I help you?"

"How are you?"

"Couldn't be better."

"I needed to hear that." He then broke into his high-pitched laughter. "Can you get to the club this weekend? We need to have a talk. Also, you were going to see about bringing your friend, Chinky?"

"You're right. I forgot to call him. I'll do that right now. I can be there. About eight o'clock or eight thirty?"

"We'll be there for you at eight. When you get there, you get there. Let me know about Chinky though because that is very important."

"Will do."

I called Chinky at work.

"Hello."

"You are becoming a very important and popular friend of mine."

"How so?"

"Can you make dinner Saturday night out at New Ken?"

"At that club?"

"Yes."

"Socko! You really get involved, don't you?"

"It's what I do for a living. Sometimes I represent corporations, too, as if you don't remember."

"I remember. That was the easiest fee you ever earned. What time and did you say Saturday?"

"Saturday at eight or eight thirty."

"Are we bringing wives?"

"Just try to leave Margie home. And do you think my woman doesn't want to have dinner?"

"Right again. I'll check to see if we have any games to attend for the kids. I think the playoffs are ending Thursday. We get a break before the next sport. I think Lisa has a volleyball or basketball game Friday but that should be it."

"I don't know how you keep track of all the games. Six kids and they are all on teams. Are you still coaching?"

"Hell, no. I'm done. Now the company just sponsors teams. I'll ask Marge but I'm sure we'll be there. Will you pick us up in the limo again?"

"Sure."

"Socko! I love traveling with my lawyer friend. See you at seven thirty, I guess."

"Make it eight."

"Done."

I then made sure that I had a date.

The other receptionist answered and sent me over to Lola.

"Will wonders ever cease? A call from a man I used to know."

"Hello, my sweet."

"Well, there's an opening line. Need to have your back scratched? Or some other parts rubbed?"

"Dinner Saturday night is the reason for the call."

"I have to wait that long to eat?"

"No, and not only no, but you will also get to eat sooner with me. As soon as I get a few items out of the way, I'll do either lunch or dinner before Saturday."

"Why not both? I have to try to maintain my strength to keep up with your demands on my body."

"Alright, alright, I'll get back to you, but Saturday is the important date."

"I'll count the moments until the next time I hear my master's voice."

The intercom interrupted my review on Mirage's case.

"Mr. DiAngelo, Mrs. Parks on the phone."

"Carole Rae, how are you?"

"I'm fine, Lou. Leo told me you needed some info on the New York property."

"Right. I need the rental agent's name and who you may have allowed to use the property."

"The rental agent is with ReMax. I don't remember their names. We didn't have any one person. They all worked on renting the property."

"One of your cousins used it?"

"Yes, Gary Garofalo was up there a couple of times. He went up with the guys to get away, play poker, drink beer and generally goof off."

"Do you know where he is now?"

"As a matter of fact, I don't. The last I heard he was out in Nevada somewhere, probably went to Vegas if he spent any time there. Probably visited with the guys from the avenue that work out there, I don't know. Rulli and Alex are still there. Dodson died, Ciuffe died."

"Yeah, I know. No other idea where he might be?"

"No."

"Any idea when he was there?"

"As a matter of fact, it was the Fourth of July, last year, and then the end of September, last year."

"Good, thank you."

"Why do you need all this?"

"I'm sorry, I thought Leo would have told you. The U.S. Attorney in New York found some items that are questionable and he was checking up. I am trying to make sure that he doesn't look to you and Leo for any reason. You know about the U.S. Attorney?"

"Yes, Leo told me about the subpoena."

"Well, that's the reason."

"Are we safe? I mean do we have anything to worry about?"

"Not if you have told me everything. So far you have done nothing wrong."

"Thank God! I don't need any more headaches or heartaches."

"Okay. Take care. I'll let you know if anything else comes up."

I called U.S. Attorney Robinson and provided him all the information that I had. He was appreciative and seemed somewhat satisfied. but I was sure that he would now have the FBI follow up to get interviews and a handle on what he is pursuing.

"Mr. D, two detectives here."

"Villalpando and Bruno?"

"Yes, sir."

"I'll be right out."

"Gentlemen, come in. Did she offer you coffee or water or whatever?"

"She did. That could be reason enough to come see you. The coffee is always good."

"Especially for you so that we can bribe you with java."

They both smiled and seated themselves.

"So that you know, we have some leads on Allana's murder. Did you know Joey Dee?"

"Did I? Not do I?"

"He was found in a trunk in West Virginia."

"Oh boy."

"We were able to make some matches that make us suspect he may have been the perp in the Allana case. We can make the connection but we don't know the why."

"Well, he was muscle for a lot of years."

"With the guys on the other side of the river, not up the river."

"Is that supposed to be funny?"

"I didn't mean anything about up the river, just geography. Not your clients. But maybe you hear things."

"Not about that."

"I hear you are being a good guy and keeping your people out of reach of the U.S. Attorney."

"My job is to protect my clients from the evils of the justice system. And not at the expense of my other clients. I never expose them to any known dangers."

Detective Villalpando spoke up, "We're reasonably sure that Allana knew something and she was a danger to someone's way of thinking. You are working on liquor licenses. Can you think of any connection?"

"Like if she knew someone had a past that would prevent them from getting a license? That's hardly a reason to kill somebody."

"Maybe not to you."

"You make a point but I don't think that's the case here. My guys are clean. Sam's daughter is clean."

"Sam's daughter? She's going to be the license holder?"

"That's right. Why not? It was her father's. By the way, are you guys getting anything on his case?"

"Not really looking that hard. That was his chosen profession and we figure the other members of his profession will solve that mystery for us. If not, we'll get to it eventually."

"That's refreshing."

"What do you know about crystal meth?"

"I know that it is deadly. I know that I stick with single malt scotch, for sure."

"Heard anything about any labs around here?"

"If I did I probably wouldn't be able to tell you, but my people don't do dangerous stuff like that."

"That's what they said in the Godfather movie, but when the guys see the money that turns around quickly they lose their fear of the dangerous."

"Not when they are facing all that jail time. The only people doing those labs are already hooked,"

"We heard that there are some important people in town."

"There are always a lot of important people in town. What does that mean?"

"We had a hunch that they were going to get into the meth business, Allana found out, Sam got in her way or maybe tried to protect her, Joey Dee did Sam and Allana and then they had to make sure that Joey never got around to telling anybody so he gets whacked. Neat little package."

"Neat all right. That's a great theory but I don't have any basis to believe that it's accurate. Do you guys have anything solid to support that scenario?"

"Not yet. We're starting at the meth lab as a start. Maybe if your guys were in the business they would want you to tell us about any competitors so that we would go after the competition."

"What a twisted little mind you show sometimes. Well, I guess with all the perps you have to arrest, you get to think like them sometimes."

"You don't think your people wouldn't have thought of that?"

"Yes. They did. They told me to not trust you and to tell an Irish cop because an Italian and Mexican might be the perfect pair, one covers the mob, the other covers the border."

With that, we all laughed.

"That was good. Seriously, though, if there is anything you can think of that wouldn't compromise you, let us know."

"If I could help you. By the way, did you ever talk to Allana's husband?"

"She had more than one husband. We're working on the Deacon."

"Gentlemen, I'd like to say it's been a pleasure…"

"But you won't because it wasn't, right?"

"That's a better line than the one I was going to use."

I ushered both of them out to the waiting room and went back to my cases. Looked like enough for the day.

I decided to try for a late lunch at Rico's. The traffic along McKnight was light and so was the lunch. A couple of manhattans before, pleasant chat with Rico after the salad and then the lemon sole Florentine. I decided not to go back to the office. Time to get rested for what lies ahead. Maybe a Padron 1964 or a counterfeit Cuban from JR Tobacco and a try for a good night of sleep.

CHAPTER TWENTY

Dean arrived with Lola in tow.

"Good evening, sir."

"Dean, how are you?"

"Fine, sir."

I got in the back with Lola.

"God, you look great. It seems like it's been a long time." We kissed gently.

"You smell nice? What's the scent?"

"Yves St. Laurent pour l'homme. I think I said it right."

"Close enough."

She took my hand and squeezed it gently.

"We're going to New Ken but first we have to pick up the Predmores. Do you remember where they live?"

"Yes, sir. We took them with us last time you went to the club out there. What time are you expected in New Ken?"

"In an hour. I figure you can make it to their house in thirty minutes and then to New Ken in another thirty minutes."

"What's the big meeting tonight?"

"I'm not really sure, but if I had to guess, since they want to see Chinky so much that it has to do with distribution through Daily Juice or something. Something that I wouldn't be able to tell you if I knew."

"Well, I'm happy to be able to enjoy a good meal, and at a place where I can light up with no problem."

We made pretty good time over to the next stop and even better time to the club.

"What time shall I expect to be back?"

"Between eleven thirty and midnight. I don't think anybody wants to drink all night tonight, or am I missing something, Chink?"

"Midnight is good. Who knows, you may remember how we used to come in after dawn."

"Make it midnight, Dean, he's feeling invincible, I can see. Probably he'll order the hot peppers to see if anybody winces at the spice."

"Very good, sir. See you then. I'll probably be outside twenty minutes before, just in case."

We went down the steps as Dean pulled away and Tony was quickly there to greet us.

"Hello, everybody. So glad that you could all make it again and happy to have you here."

We were ushered into the restaurant proper away from the bar and a rather well endowed creature came over to take our drink orders. She also presented a wine list.

From the back, Raphael and Tony's wife started to the table. I stood as they approached, as did Chinky.

"Sit down, no need for formality."

"We weren't standing for you. There was a lady approaching."

"Oh, I see." He looked at her, "Real gentlemen we have here tonight."

He looked back at us, "Very well. The lady will join us if you all don't mind."

Lola spoke up next.

"If you all won't mind, Marge and I will take our drinks at the bar with a cigarette. We can talk lady talk while you all do whatever it is that you do. Besides the table will be more comfortable and the smoke won't bother anyone."

"I hope you don't mind that I had Tony's wife sit in and that I asked for your friend here to come along."

"Why would I mind? We're all friends and family, no?"

"You got some mouth, you. Maybe that's why I like you."

"No, you like me because I am able to get what you want and never sacrifice my manhood."

"Now what does that mean?"

"It means that I respect you and treat you like a person, the same as I expect. Nothing more, nothing less. In addition, I produce what I am paid to produce. Finally, because I like you."

"See what I mean. Ok, enough of the back and forth. Joanne here is going to be the license holder, right?"

"Right."

"Can we sell product out of here?"

"If you're suggesting what I think, no. What are you thinking as product?"

"We're looking to get the import export license and market whiskey."

"That would be why you wanted Chinky to be here for the Daily connection?"

"Right. I know he can't sell but their company can suggest, as it were, to the places where they go, about buying certain brands, no?"

"They could. Why would they want to do that?"

"If we can make an offer to his guys, Meyer and Frank, I am sure they would consider it."

"So, essentially, you will want them to market and you are also suggesting a certain financial reward to them for helping."

"Nobody works for nothing. You attorneys know that better than anybody."

"How does that sound to you, Chink?"

"I can suggest it to them. What are we talking about?"

"Maybe some Russian imported vodka to start. We're trying to work a deal with the Jewish family from Canada that we might be able to work in as well."

"I'll ask."

"That's all I can expect. Anything from you, Joanne?"

"No, I'm happy to be sure that I have some control and if the license is in my name and I have an interest in the import export business, what more could a girl want?"

"Good. Then it's all agreed. Enjoy yourselves. The night's on us."

They both got up and walked away. He had his arm around her shoulder and was very attentive.

"How come no Tony in the discussion?"

"Very good, Charlie. You noticed."

"I never knew about wives doing business without the husband."

"Maybe it's the new age. There are a lot of wives that are smarter than their husbands."

Lola and Marge approached, "Were you just now talking about us?"

"Maybe his wife. You're just a friend."

"I'll remember that later."

"Does that mean you won't be friendly?"

"Careful, Buster, you're liable to start walking with a limp."

"Now, that wouldn't be to anybody's benefit, would it?"

"Maybe it would help me make a choice that I might need to stop putting off…"

"How about a choice for what you want to eat and drink for tonight, okay?"

"You two having a go-round again?"

"Not really, she's just showing me how much she loves me."

"I'll have the filet if the love talk is over. Marge?"

"I'll have the surf and turf."

"Veal parmesan for me."

"As usual for you, Charlie."

"I'll have the New York Strip, okay miss?" She took the rest of the order and everything went fine with small talk and cigars and cigarettes.

Tony came over from the office in back and sat near me, "Everything all right with the dinner?"

Everybody went on how good everything had been.

He then leaned toward me, "Meeting go okay?"

"Fine. Why do you ask and why weren't you sitting in on it?"

"Not my game. The wife is the name. I am the manager. The imports are the old man's."

"You know about the vodka?"

"More than anybody."

"It looks like a good idea if the merchandising and the distribution moves well. Right, Chink?"

"It will depend if the purveyors and retailers pick up on it. They're all the same. If it works, good. If not, it was a good idea that didn't click."

We listened to some music and left right on time, just before midnight. Dean was at the curb, "The evening all finished, sir?"

"Depends on the lady."

Chinky and Marge smiled to each other as Lola glanced up at me.

"The lady is tired. I did bring an overnight bag, but if it's all the same to you, I think I'll sleep in my own bed tonight. I'll miss having you make me breakfast but I do have some errands to run tomorrow."

The smiles disappeared.

"I understand."

Chinky was most interested in what had happened at the club.

"I wonder if Meyer will go for it. He is a very close to the vest businessman. He won't risk anything that might have a down side and blow up in his face, so to speak, and with these guys it may not just be a figure of speech."

"Are you going to ask about it?"

"Why not? He's a big boy. He can make up his own mind. I'll just put out what happened and ask if he wants me to do any reviews. I'm not sure there is anything to review as of yet, anyhow."

"When they were young, nothing was too risky, but after you accumulate a little bit of wealth the tendency is to protect what you have. Let me know what they say as it may affect what I do for these guys."

"Will do."

We dropped of Marge and Chinky and proceeded to my house.

"Is this good night?"

"It is. Not goodbye. I truly am exhausted and I'll save a couple of hours if I go straight home."

We kissed gently.

"Maybe we could do something together tomorrow after I get all my stuff done?"

"Why not. I'll go home with the morning paper tonight and cuddle up in the headlines as this might make front page news… prominent attorney shot down by significant other."

"Oh, Christ, just pretend that we're married. Married couples always have more important things to do than make love. Like cook and clean, get their nails, hair and other parts done. Just be happy you aren't getting a bikini wax. You couldn't handle it."

"On that note, you win. If you can sit up straight after your 'errands', I'll take you out again tomorrow. We could do lunch at Bob's Garage, early dinner at Girasole's or dinner at Morton's. It will be your choice as you had to dine out at this place tonight."

"I do love you. Even though you piss me off sometimes, you always seem to try to make it up."

"Last chance to change your mind."

"Tempting, but no. Dean can take me home, thanks. I'll see you tomorrow. Tonight wasn't bad."

We kissed a little less gently and they left.

I went in and headed straight for the downstairs bar for a Strega and a short cigar. A Padron 1964 vintage. I clicked on the television to watch CNN and switched between there and the late rerun of local news. My emergency service buzzed on my cell.

"Mr. DiAngelo, we have a message from a Mr. Mirage. He's been picked up and is in custody. He called the office and was forwarded to your emergency site."

"Any other info?"

"Yes, it was the United States Marshal Service. They weren't going to let him make any calls but the marshal knew you and allowed the call. He's downtown."

"Well, there's nothing I can do tonight. Thank you. Was there a phone number?"

"The Marshal's office phone."

I took the number. I called and was transferred.

"Hello, Luig?"

"Hello. Thank you. To whom do I have the pleasure of speaking?"

"This is Gene."

"Gene? Oh, Gene. I forgot you were there."

"Ouch. You hurt me. All these years I worked my way up, and thanks to you and the guy in your office for those calls way back when I was able to move up. Ok, so you forgot. Never mind, I still remember. Anyway, I understand we have one of your guys here."

"That's right. A Mr. Mirage."

"He's your client, right?"

"Right."

"Hasn't been sentenced yet but he is going to need a toothbrush, right?"

"Right. Am I going to win a prize for answering all these questions correctly?"

"No, but Mr. Mirage is about to win a prize. His life."

"What does that mean?"

"Is this a secure phone line?"

"I don't know. I don't check them. I usually don't discuss any secrets on the phone."

"Your guy is about to go to the can, meet with some people, get some information, have you file for a review and, in addition, or maybe all by itself, file for early release, commutation or whatever you attorneys do to get these upstanding citizens back on the street. He will and you know it."

"Wait a minute. You're getting a little ahead of me. He hasn't even gone to the can yet."

"He will and you know it. You knew it from the beginning and the friend of yours that told you so was right. They need him in the can to get the info. Then he kills the guy, actually the guy dies accidentally while on a work detail, a backhoe falls over on him. You get your guy out, he provides all the info and then he disappears. Clean as a whistle. Nobody to talk. Just like all the hits. The hitter also gets hit so nobody can follow the ladder. Fortunately for your guy, the judge's phone isn't secure either. The government has been looking at this judge for some time and had it wired. There were some conversations that you might like. Most of it was favorable to you but some of the guys thought that you were a smartass and needed to have a loser to bring you back to earth. Not my feeling, of course, but maybe they know you better than me."

"Cute."

"Not my business. Hey, didn't I get you the info? Not everybody gets a call. Anyway, we have him in protective custody, he won't go to the can, he will be offered the witness protection program and we will let him hear the transcripts of other conversations where their plot is to whack him after he gets the info and has the other guy buried. Now, do I have your attention?"

"What's your next step?"

"He'll be here. You can ask for bond, but you won't get it. You can see him to act as his attorney but I can't guarantee the fee. I can assure you that he's not going anywhere. We have a pretty sharp U.S. Attorney on the case, Attorney Smith. He has us all taking precautions and the court on notice. I can give you his number but Saturday night you can be sure he's not in the office."

"Wait a minute. You're with the U.S. Marshal. In fact, you are the U.S. Marshal, but that doesn't allow you to tap phones."

"Right you are. Don't you think that we get information from other branches? That we work together on investigations? Let me go even one better. The U.S. Attorney was investigating another judge. A friend of yours who is dating another judge. Bells ringing? Well, the tap went on the wrong phone line and they get the judge on this Mirage case by mistake. While recording, guess what conversation they get? Bingo! So, now they have a basis for a real tap."

"Why tap on my friend?"

"Because his girlfriend uses things that aren't legal. It would be nice to have that lead. Also to get a judge provides big headlines for those wishing to move up in the political world. Makes them look like a 'law and order' candidate. In the meantime, they get all kinds of good stuff. Your guy is the beneficiary of all this. We, that is the FBI and this office, are able to learn that your guy plays poker every Saturday night with some very interesting people. We came in during the game. He was really pissed as he was holding a flush with a big pot. We left the guys to split the pot when we escorted him out. He has enough on him to pay a small retainer, but, like I said, he's not going anywhere. Nice to talk to you, my friend. Anything else I can sell you tonight?"

"Gene, I really appreciate the information. I'll have to explain to the judge why he can't appear for sentencing."

"The judge may ask you why the feds have him. What are you going to tell him?"

"That he is in protective custody with the Federal government, U.S. Marshal's office and that the judge will have to inquire if he wants anything further."

"Good. I confided in you. You didn't take an oath but you know the game. If you did open up, I might never be able to trust you again. If that happened, well, you know."

"I do know and I appreciate it. Thanks. Now I hope I can get some sleep with all this information working on my mind."

"You mean you take cases like this seriously?"

"If you represent people, you get into their body and suffer. Also, nobody likes to lose. Good night, buddy. Make sure to lock all the doors."

"Take care, Luigi. Always good to talk to you."

My God! How things happen! What a deal. I'll have to try to sort this all out tomorrow. Good thing Lola went home. I would have been preoccupied and who knows whether I could have performed. Who's kidding who? She would have made sure that I was able to perform. I never met a woman that couldn't make a guy get excited in spite of all the television ads for erectile dysfunction.

CHAPTER
TWENTY-ONE

The day didn't look too bad. Made some Gevalia breakfast blend coffee, a couple of poached eggs with sausage and read the Sunday paper in bed. Finally got up at eleven, got ready and to church.

"Hey Buon Giorno, Luigi. Come esta?"

"Bene. Aren't you in an upbeat mood today?"

"Hey, I'm on the right side of the grass. The sun's out, the people are here and even you showed up. Do you need me to hear your confession real quick?"

"No. Unfortunately, it's been a slow week. No hookers, no extortions. I can't even get a sheep to stay the night. Does murder still count?"

"Shame on you. Good thing I know you kid a lot."

"What? You think the sheep are making a comeback?"

"Stop it. Somebody's liable to hear you."

"Don't worry. I'll pray real loud and they'll think I'm a saint. How are you doing?"

"I'm fine. I even have a new assistant. Father Tom Speracino. He's a nice local kid from up north of I-80. Breaking him into how parishes work. Shows some promise, but who knows? I think the bishop has an eye on him. Probably keep him here for a while then send him to the suburbs to burn off the baby fat and have him find the real work of saving souls in a parish."

"Hey, we all have our crosses to bear. Isn't that what the good book says?"

"Oh, you're going to throw scripture back in my face? Get inside, we have to get started."

All priests should be as down to earth as Father Carmine.

After services, I called Lola.

"Interested in doing anything today?"

"With you?"

"Ouch. What did I do to deserve that?"

"I think it's just the relationship. I'm not sure what it will ever turn out to be."

"What did I promise you?"

"That's a horrible thing to say. And that's probably what I mean. You never promised anything. You are always attentive and enjoyable but are you ever going to be mine? I mean really mine."

"Do you know how many divorces I handle? Do you know all the shit I see everyday? I do my best to make a wonderful lady happy and, I think, I do pretty well at succeeding, but you call me on the carpet and complain. Will a piece of paper and a reception make all that much of a difference? You realize that there will be a pre-nup and how will that make you feel? Better that you are now married, but that your husband thought about the legal ramifications beforehand? I'm not an impulsive guy, but I am getting angry. I do all I can and if it isn't good enough for you, then you're right. You're shopping in the wrong store. Now you have made me regret the call. Before I say anything that we might, and I say might, both regret, I'll call you later. I think I'll call you later is even better."

I turned on the television and poured a Macallan 25. I was happy because 25 I sip and don't fire down. It would calm me down a little.

The phone rang.

"Hello."

"Can we talk?"

"Are we still talking?"

"Can I come over right now? I want to say that I'm sorry."

"You just did."

"Not in words."

"I'm a little upset. No, I'm a lot upset. You know, or should know, how much you mean to me and you should know me well enough to know you got me pissed real good. Of course, I always like to see you but I can't promise I'll be such a nice guy because I'm still steaming."

"I'll be there in thirty." And she hung up the phone.

Even though it was a bit chilly, I went out on the deck with the drink to air my anger out. A car pulled into the driveway. It was the Greek.

"Mr. D, I hope you don't get mad at me. I was asked if I could get to you. Those guys don't know where you live. I wouldn't tell them which got them a little upset so I had to make some moves to keep them happy. They need to talk to you regarding the Mirage deal. Also, I needed to know when you want to have me at your office tomorrow for the pardon app?"

"Come on up, Steve. Can I fix you a drink?"

"I'm not much of a drinker. I'll have what you're having."

"No, you won't. If you're not a drinker, I'm not wasting this on you. What so you usually drink?"

"Scotch on the rocks with a splash."

"Got it, Johnny Walker Black ok?"

"Good deal."

"Now, what?"

"The guys need to talk to you. You know they picked up Mirage last night?"

"I do know."

"Do you think that maybe you ought to call them?"

"Why? What good is that going to do?"

"It will make them feel better if they hear from you."

"They're not my clients."

"They put up the twenty though, didn't they?"

"Sometimes I get checks from clients that were loans from banks or ATMs. I don't answer to banks or ATMs either."

"Mr. D, I'm your friend, remember me. Why do you want to work me over?"

"It's Sunday, my day of rest. I have this bullshit, I get calls from the U.S. Marshall late at night and my lady friend is pulling a snit. All this and I haven't had lunch yet."

"Ok, I apologize. I'm just doing my job. Come to think of it, I'm a day early, aren't I? The argument on my case is tomorrow. Do me a favor. Here's the number. At least call them after you have lunch, or make up with your girlfriend, or whatever. I'll tell them that I gave you the info. You were busy but that you would try to get to them. Thanks, Counselor."

"You be at my office tomorrow at nine o'clock."

"See you then."

I wondered whether to call now or after I had lunch. Figured it might be easier on my stomach if I called before I ate.

The number looked familiar as I dialed it. Then again, all the numbers start to look familiar.

"Louie, honey."

"Rosa?"

"Yes, sweetie. Thanks for calling. Can we talk on the phone?"

"I'm not going to say anything that can be used against me."

"Honey, what can you tell me about Mirage?"

"The U.S. Marshall has him. They have him in custody. He will be told information that the feds have and they will offer him the witness protection program."

"What do they have?"

"That I don't really know. They have information that Mirage was going into the can to get info from an inmate, and then kill the inmate. It would be an accident. A backhoe would fall on him. Then Mirage was supposed to be released on a commutation from the sentencing judge after my motion for a new trial gets a favorable review. He would get time served and be free. Only the feds overheard on a wire that revealed Mirage wasn't going to get out alive. He was going to be killed as well to be sure no one could finger the man pulling the strings. Who that might be is not certain to me and I'm not sure the government is either."

"Thanks, sweetheart. When am I going to see you up at the restaurant?"

"I don't get up that way too often anymore but thanks for the invitation."

"Thank you for all the help. I'll be talking to you."

I went over to the kitchen and looked for something for lunch in the refrigerator. I heard the garage door opening. I looked out the window and saw a familiar Cadillac in the driveway.

"Am I too late for lunch?"

"Who invited you?"

"Did I deserve that? Ok, maybe I did a little. I came over to say I'm sorry in person. Over the phone would have been tough and I wasn't sure that you would have answered, and I am sorry." With that she rushed up and threw her arms around me, kissing me feverishly and endlessly. Suddenly, I knew that lunch was going to have an appetizer that would take all the tension out of my body. I was trying to stay angry with her, but, like Charlie said on Two and a Half Men, make-up sex is one of the great pleasures that comes your way. Makes you think that maybe it is smart to start arguments just to have make-up sex. After we each made sure that the other had all the pleasure they could stand on an empty stomach, we started to get put back together.

"You know I am really sorry about the blowup. I hope that you understand that women are different from men and that we feel things differently."

"Vive la difference."

"I did feel badly after but I do feel for you and want so much of you that I guess I let my thoughts go dark and wondered if I didn't have you someone else might."

"What makes you think permanent is really permanent."

"I'd like to try."

"Ask Father Carmine. You must be working for his team the way you talk."

"Did you see Father Carmine today?"

"Yes, I did, as a matter of fact."

"How is he?"

"He's fine. He has some wiseass kid from New Castle working with him. He thinks he's a spy for the bishop or that he's leapfrogging to get into the big buck contributor group. He seemed like a nice enough kid, but what do I know?"

"Can we get lunch?"

"What's your pleasure?"

"Sunday afternoon, how about that old standby, Bob's Garage?"

We got put together and headed for lunch.

Nice group of people were at the bar. Meghan was on duty and moving to and fro. Bob was there and he came over.

"How's my favorite attorney?"

"I wouldn't know. I haven't seen him for a long time."

"Come on, Lou, how are you doing? Of course, I should know, 'Couldn't be better'."

"You got it. How's everything with you and yours?"

"Same old, you know. But your name did come up recently."

"How so?"

"Two detectives were in. They were working up the case on Allana."

"Did they say that they had anything going on the case?"

"Asked me if I had seen any foreign sounding or looking guys."

"Really? I wonder why?"

"I did too. I didn't think it had anything to do with illegals from Mexico, I can assure you. They were decent about it, though, pleasant enough."

"I guess as much as you can be with a nasty murder."

The rest of lunch went well and we headed back to my place.

"I should have told you to follow me. It would have made your trip home a bit shorter."

"But it also would have made my time with you shorter."

She slid her hand affectionately up and down my leg. "I could make do with what I have in the car and not have to drive all that long, long drive home."

"It didn't occur to you that it was so long getting here did it."

"I practically flew."

"I must confess that I am glad that you did. I have some court appearances tomorrow and you know how to lock up if I leave before you."

"We'll be fine and I take that as a 'yes, I can stay the night'."

"Of course. Do I look like the kind of guy that would throw out a beautiful lady that can perform like you do."

"Yes, but so long as it's all the other ones that you throw out."

We had leftovers for dinner, watched a movie and spent a peaceful end to the day.

CHAPTER TWENTY-TWO

"Are we missing something, Mr. DiAngelo?"

"Yes, your Honor."

"Would you care to enlighten us? I'm sure we are all ears and can't wait to hear why you are not in the company of the wonderful people you represent."

"Well, your Honor, Mr. Mirage is now in the company as well as the custody of the United States government. I received information over the weekend that he is in protective custody. He may or may not be a key witness to what has apparently been an ongoing investigation for some period of time. I really don't know much else except that the U.S. Marshall's office has him."

"You're serious?"

"Nobody kids about a missing client at time of sentence or when the feds are involved."

"Does the District Attorney's office have any position that they would like to make clear?"

"Your Honor, Mr. DiAngelo had reported as accurately as we are able to determine. I can't add anything to what he has just said other than we should consider continuing the sentencing to a future date pending the physical presence of the defendant."

"Court will be adjourned until a future date as may meet the schedule of all involved. Mr. DiAngelo, I'd like to see you in chambers on another matter, if you don't mind."

"I have a commutation hearing at 10:30 downstairs, your Honor. So long as I am able to appear on time."

"You will, I am sure."

I went out of the courtroom and through the secretary's area to enter the chambers.

"Sit down, Lou. I need to talk to you about the Mirage matter aside from the sentencing. I understand that you are handling a Partition case with Attorneys Tunney and Pukalski."

"That's correct, your Honor, Judge Bartolomeo assigned me to the case. We've had the first meeting and I have the case calendared in for later this month."

"Good. I may need you to represent me in relation to the U.S. government."

"I beg your pardon. What is the connection?"

"I am taking over the Partition case responsibility. Judge Bartolomeo was kind enough to allow me to preside."

"I still don't understand… Maybe I am missing some…"

"Get real, Lou. I have the Partition case, you need to have your fees approved, you can charge any additional amount that you need and I will approve the request and then you will have your fee for representing me. I know what the cases with the United States government cost and I am only a local judge. I don't have that kind of money."

"What are you saying?"

"I received the required notice of a wiretap. I have also been advised that I am more than a person of interest. I am being considered as a target."

"I'm sorry to hear that, your Honor, but I can't do what you are asking. Not that I wouldn't like to help you, but I couldn't do it free or for a million dollars. The U.S. Attorney will conflict me out. I have the star witness as my client, all the information I have from him will be confidential and can't be brought up by me to defend you or even inquire about your case. I'm sorry, Judge. I'd like to help but I am the last guy that could get involved. I'll forget about the offer on the Partition case as though that was something said in haste and unintentional."

"Who do you think I should ask?"

"Bobby DelGreco, Jimmy Wymard, Michael DeRiso. There are a ton of attorneys that would be happy to help you out. I wish I could, but sorry."

I made my way out of his chambers. As I glanced back at him, I could see the end of his life going before him. All because of his involvement with another judge and her bad habits.

I took the steps down to the third floor. Standing in front of the courtroom was the Greek.

"Good morning, Counselor."

"Hello, Steve."

"Are we early?"

"I don't know. I'll have to see the list." I went into the courtroom and picked up the list. We were sixth on the list. I recognized the attorney on the case being argued and he was on the third case. We had two more and then to us. I took a seat and watched the proceedings. The Lieutenant Governor was his usual receptive self. The Attorney General was doing most of the questioning.

Before too long, our case was called. I presented the future employer, the character witnesses and finally, the Greek. He was surprisingly charming, or else the fact that the board were old friends of mine allowed the proceedings to go as smoothly as possible.

The District Attorney's office made the usual arguments against and outlined how the Greek had not been fully rehabilitated by not having lengthy employment at one place over the years.

The Attorney General responded that employment was one of the reasons the Pardon was being requested, to allow a full time position in automobile sales by obtaining a license to sell. We then recessed.

"How did I do, Counselor?"

"You did real well. It's almost a cinch from what we saw. But you know I'm never certain about anything until I see it in my hands."

"Thanks, I owe you."

"You don't owe me anything. You paid up front."

"You know what I meant. How long before we hear anything?"

"Figure sixty days. They have to review all the sides of the argument and then write an opinion. It takes a little time. Don't worry, it will be soon enough."

We parted and I headed for the office. What a morning.

"Messages for you, Mr. D."

I took the messages with me into the office. I had to call three different numbers until I finally got Charlie Caputo on his cell.

"When are you going to get your office phone straightened out?"

"I don't know. We're working on it. What can I do for you in the meantime?"

"I am returning your call."

"I took a look at that transfer for you and called Harrisburg. It looks like it will sail through. Her father may have had problems but she is clean as new fallen snow. Shouldn't be a problem to get it all the way quickly. The import and hotel licenses are a little different, but I still don't have all the information needed for the apps as the corporations are not formed and the officers are not picked out. How did you get so many requests at the same time?"

"That's why I called you. I have a million things going so I needed extra typing hands. I still have to get the corporation formed for the hotel deal."

"Well, I just wanted to let you know so that you can tell the clients."

"Thanks, Charlie. What would you like for money?"

"Maybe about four thousand. Get a big retainer. We can always make a refund."

"That'll be the day."

I thought that I had better get going on the Partition case before the judge found a lawyer willing to go to jail for accepting payments from an inflated billing. Mail fraud would be the least of the problems that they would face. I shook my head and I sent out the notice fixing the hearing date.

"Mr. DiAngelo, U.S. Attorney Smith on the phone."

"Send it through."

"Hello."

"Hello, Mr. DiAngelo. This is the United States Attorney Smith. I am calling you regarding a person that I think that you represent."

"Yes, I know, Mr. Mirage."

"That's right, but you know I have a bit of a problem with his name. I find a Dellacroce that comes up with his social security number. Can you explain why that is?"

"I'm not sure. I do know that he felt he had to change his name for some reason. I don't think he told me why. Oh, you know what, I think it was because his father or uncle was a police officer. Are you sure you guys didn't change it before and he is already in the witness protection from a prior incident?"

The U.S. Attorney even laughed at that.

"You know, back when they were doing all the capos in New York, that became a real possibility. The real reason I called you is that we want to take statements from him and we want to be sure that the right to counsel doesn't get raised against us in any fashion. Will you be able to get with him some time in the near future?"

"I suppose I can make arrangements on my calendar. When are visiting hours and do you have facilities for an attorney to meet with his client?"

"We would have to make arrangements for you to meet with him in our offices. You realize that we can't have his whereabouts become public knowledge."

"I understand."

"Why don't you see what your calendar allows for a meeting time and let me know and I can make arrangements or see what other time will be good for everybody."

"Sounds like a plan. Let me put you back with my staff and they will get your contact info."

"That will be fine. You should know that your client is very involved and will be very useful against some very prominent people. I want you to be aware of what we will be asking when he agrees after consulting with his attorney."

"If he agrees."

"I'm fairly confident he will. If we don't protect him, who will stop the people that want him dead from making it happen?"

"You make a point."

I sent him back to the staff and looked at what I needed to get finished.

"Mr. DiAngelo, Detectives Bruno and Villalpando are here."

I came out of the office, "Don't you guys ever call before you come calling?"

"We try to catch the people we talk to off guard."

"Very funny. You're just lucky that you caught me between cases. Come in and sit down."

They sat and Bruno started.

"We think we have something going on Allana's murder. Did you know her ex-husband?"

"Yes, I knew him way back when. I think I would still remember him."

"Did you know that he was making moves along the border between New York and Pennsylvania?"

"The Deac? No, I wouldn't have guessed that."

Villalpando chimed in, "You know a guy called Toto?"

"I know the name. I've probably even met him but I really don't remember him. By the way, you haven't read me my rights so I am assuming this is not targeted questioning but merely a fact finding visit."

"As far as we are concerned, you are clean and only represent dirt."

"Careful. I also represent more than a few police officers. But then again, you might be right."

"Fair enough, I take that back."

"There's good and bad everywhere, as we know."

"Back to the info. Allana had your retainer on her when she came in. She told you that her husband wasn't paying anything. We find out that he was making trips to New York and meeting with Toto in Oakmont and in Oakland as well as Bloomfield. Also spent a couple of nights in New Kensington. You also represent Leo Parks, right?"

"Right now regarding property that is in New York."

"The place has been inspected and traces of meth were found."

"I heard that before."

"And the real estate agent was found dead nearby."

"Is there going to be something you are going to tell me?"

"We think all these items are connected. We have the feds, DEA and Immigration all interested in the New York house and we think Allana found out something."

"From whom?"

"Not sure but we think all these dots connect and that she wasn't telling you the whole truth about her husband's income."

Villalpando chimed in again, "We also came across your client Mirage. He's in protective custody and probably will supply a lot of info to the feds. We hear there was a contract for him to handle and then he was the next contract. To be sure no one could get back to the person calling the shots."

"So, you see we have been accumulating a lot of info that we need to connect. Especially since Leo is married into the family and the word is that a motel and import export license, liquor license and imported vodka is to be distributed using Daily Juice route distribution. Meyer and Frankie at Daily's wouldn't get involved unless it promised a good payday and no exposure. We know that they retired when the legitimate business paid off."

"We just don't know who pulled the triggers."

"As an attorney, don't you have a duty to make a report to prevent a crime from happening?"

"That's right, I do, but I don't know of anything that is suspicious enough to make me look to the authorities."

"Who's pushing for the import export?"

"I can't tell you anything about my cases or my clients, you know that."

He then leaned over to Villalpando, "He was cited for contempt by the U.S. Attorney for failure to reveal and the Court quashed the attempt. Mr. DiAngelo had his toothbrush with him. The judge told the U.S. Attorney that this was a sham since they knew he wasn't going to talk and they subpoenaed him anyway. Same thing here again?" he directed to me.

"You know it is. That's not what is bothering me though. I am bothered by the fact that you guys know more than me and I am the trusted one. Not the enemy."

"That depends on your point of view. Attorneys are a necessary evil to guys that do the things we investigate. It's like nobody likes the police until they are in danger or it looks like they need help. Then all of a sudden the men in blue are like saints."

"We have something in common then. Attorneys are not on the top ten of most admired until your son or daughter gets arrested for drugs or DUI or worse. Then they light candles until the case is over. One way or another until the next time."

"The one thing you could help us with is the New York house and who the contact for the license are going to be at the end."

"I can tell you, as a matter of public record, that Sam's daughter will be the licensee applicant."

"Tony's wife, too, isn't she?"

"That's also a matter of public record."

"The import export will be a corporation Ocivres."

"The officers?"

"I can't tell you but it will be on the PA Corporate website after the papers are filed."

"That's fair enough. Thanks for all your time."

With that they left. Another wonderful day was unfolding.

I saw that the morning had turned to afternoon already. I was a little beat up as I had been in two different courts, propositioned by a judge, approached by the U.S. Attorney and visited by the Pittsburgh detectives. I guess the FBI and Immigration had more important things to do. So did I. One of them was to get something to eat. I decided to head up to a local bistro, Tavern 245, right up the street. They could get you in and out, food was decent and they stocked Macallan 18 year old. Smoking at the bar with the cutest young bartenders all made for a slam-dunk.

Gina was working the bar. She and Amanda were exchanging places to keep the food and drinks moving. I had a Macallan as opposed to the Manhattan and the Ham and Cheese. It was really prosciutto and brick cheese with honey mustard served on a sourdough roll. Hungry men real time eating. It was enjoyable to watch the investment brokers at the bar. They come to lunch together, break out their smart phones, eat and work, heads down and keep company with only the latest data reports. I must confess though, they hear everything that is said at the bar.

The construction workers, on the other hand, enjoy their food and really take a break. No shop talk. Only sports and social topics along with food, beer and cigarettes. Nice to have a place where the suits and ties and work boots can smoke together without feeling uneasy at either their choices or their company. Possibly the Tavern 245 owners made sure that the clientele always behaved well enough to keep it all in good order.

I finished up and headed back to the office. It was gray and cloudy. I was contented and didn't mind. I just wondered if I would get the Partition hearing paperwork all in order and when I was scheduled by my staff to meet with Mirage at the U.S. Attorney's office.

CHAPTER
TWENTY-THREE

"Good morning. I'm Attorney DiAngelo. I'm expected."

"Yes, sir. You can go right in."

The U.S. Attorney was waiting behind his desk. He barely looked up. A childish attempt to make himself seem important. I sat down without being asked and pulled out my phone to check on emails and any messages. He looked up.

"Oh, good morning, Attorney DiAngelo. Please… uh, make yourself comfortable."

"I didn't want to disturb your reading material so I already did make myself comfortable. Shall we get on with the events of the day?"

"Certainly. I am having Mr. Mirage brought to the attorney conference room down the hall. You realize that you are not to ask your client about his physical accommodations and that you will keep this meeting as confidential as you are able. I have a form for you to sign that indicates that no promises have been made to you or your client to allow and arrange this meeting."

"Not a problem."

"Thank you. Follow me."

We left and proceeded down the hall to the conference room. He left me alone and soon enough Mr. Mirage entered from the door on the opposite end from where I had entered.

"Mr. DiAngelo!! Great to see you!"

"And a good morning to you."

"Did they tell you what was going on?"

"I know that you are in protective custody. I'm not sure what else. They want me here to be sure that you are represented by counsel in the event that you tell them anything."

"What do you think I should do?"

"I don't know without you telling me what happened."

"I was in a card game. The feds came in with the deputies from the Sheriff's office. They broke up the game which wasn't all that important and scattered everybody, but the feds took me alone outside, put me in a car and then the U.S. Marshal's office was involved. They told me that they knew that I was supposed to go into the can, pull a hit after I got the information and that I would be whacked that night in my cell by the guards or one of the other inmates. This way I could never testify as to who was behind the killing and why I was there. That's not the way it was set up for me. I was supposed to make the hit, get cleared as self-defense and that the judge would reverse based on your briefs and whatever. It wasn't going that way. This is what they tell me. They told me they have it all on tape. I haven't heard it, but that's what they say. I just don't know what I should do. What do you think?"

"The first thing you have to consider is what are your options. What crime will they charge you with committing? What happens if you walk out? Will anybody still want to have you whacked since you couldn't get the job done? Will they want you out of the way so you could never tell who wanted you to do what? What crimes can they have removed from you? What will be the quality of life if you live? I don't have all those answers but those are all the questions for the moment."

"They told me that they are going to take care of me. Set me up with a new life. Get me a new identity. I'll get an income."

"An income only as long as they have you as a witness. You will have to find a job. They may be able to get you some kind of work, but this will mean that you will no longer be running with the wise guys. You will be driving a truck or digging ditches, or, what else are you qualified to do and still remain out of the way and out of sight?"

"I used to drive a cab. I used to sell cars. I could probably make a living."

"Otherwise, you are going to jail. They may still have somebody waiting for you there. What does anybody in the joint have to lose for killing you? Unfortunately for you, nothing."

"So you think I should go for it?"

"That's a decision you have to make. I can't advise you to turn evidence. It may be my clients that you will be providing evidence against. I think it boils down to this… you are either going to jail as you have been convicted and sentenced. The judge could still reverse himself but I don't think he will now.

You will then have to live in the can knowing that possibly someone is waiting to get you. If you talk, you will never see any of your friends or family again, but you will have a new life somewhere. Probably out west. They might try to get to you, but you will have a better chance to stay alive. Or you can be a tough guy and take your chances in jail."

"What do you think my chances are in jail?"

"Not good. I hate to tell you but drug overdoses and backhoes have a habit of killing people that have information that might be harmful to people on the outside."

"Can you help me with the prosecutor?"

"Probably a little, but not too much. These guys are pretty stiff pricks."

"See what you can do."

"You also have to understand that they will want you to waive your right to remain silent before they offer you a deal. They wanted me here to make it official."

"Yeah, yeah, I know. Let me think it over and then I'll tell them what I want to do. Ask them to let me think about it for a day or two."

I opened the door and the U.S. Marshal was quick to escort him away.

Another guard asked me to go back to see the U.S. Attorney to conclude the day. I went back, discussed the possibilities and got him to agree to immunity and to have the convictions vacated as the judge was now a target and they were working with the District Attorney. It seemed all in good order. There really wasn't anything that I did that was out of the ordinary but it was almost like a stage play in high school. You get your cues from the procedures and then make all the right comments. The end result would be that a man would live to see another day, live to tell the jury or juries what went on and maybe live to a ripe old age. Look at Henry Hill. "Great country, America," he said. He erote a book after turning and they even made a movie about him. He only mentioned his contact in Pittsburgh in passing but he spent a lot of time here, especially with Augie and Primo. Oh, well, this kid probably won't see himself on the silver screen. After meetings like this you want to shower and have a steam bath to get all the dirt off you. You get a killer off so that other killers won't kill him. He will get a chance to rehab himself. Who knows, it might even work.

I got back to the office, looked through the mail and saw that the approval had gone through. The sales agreement for the motel had been formalized by the seller. It was fifty pages long and covered every possibility I am sure but the review would wait for another day.

Billy was on the line as was Filo. Both were interested in the motel situation. I advised of the agreement to each of them and that I would provide to them after I review and make comments on a copy for them. They would then be able to consider and make a decision as to what they may wish to change or any items of question.

"Mr. DiAngelo, call from a Joe Chic."

"I hear that Sally Mirage is in custody. I hear he didn't appear for sentencing. I hear the Marshal's office has him in custody. What do you say?"

"I say you hear real well and your ears are probably burning."

"What does that mean? Don't you get cute with me you mother fuckin' attorney, who the fuck do you think you are, you weasel cock…"

"Mr. Chic, I think you are confusing me with somebody else. You are upset and you are screaming at the first person in front of you. What or why would you possibly be raising your voice and yelling at me and calling me names. Get a grip."

"You fucking attorneys are all the same. You never get upset and we do the time, pay the money, and what do we get for all that?"

"I told you from the beginning that this was a tough case to win. That it didn't look good. That when Danny took the stand, the man from the clerk's office, that it looked like the nail in the coffin. From what my informers tell me, you guys wanted him in the can anyhow. Now the feds got wind, somebody, not me because I didn't know, tipped off the U.S. Attorney that Mirage was going to be whacked. The feds saw a chance to step in and get a real good look at what was going on behind the scenes. They have him and he is being offered witness protection. In addition, the judge who heard the case will probably be indicted very shortly as they had a tap on his phone as well. The funny thing is the tap was a mistake, or so they say, but I think it is true. This is one royal pile of shit. You guys better not have been talking to the judge by phone or they probably have you on the tape as well. The hits just keep on coming."

"Listen, I'm sorry, but you know I am going to have to answer for all of this."

"It isn't even all in yet. The final score is yet to come. If Mirage talks, and I don't know how much he knows, it might be front page for a year as a steady parade of characters are brought in for questioning, take the fifth, get indicted and who knows what else."

"On another note, how's the import deal going?"

"Should have it next week."

"Is the deal with Daily's coming along?"

"The last time I talked with Chinky he said Meyer was going along for a piece of the action."

"Those fucking Jews are always looking for a piece."

"Not like Italians, I guess, is that what you're saying?"

"Don't get me worked up again."

"Listen, whether Jewish, German, Gentile or Muslim, everybody looks to make a profit. It's the American way. You give me mine, I give you yours. I think Meyer is going to ask for distribution costs and ten percent of what he collects along the route. In short, you will pay for delivery, which will include delivery of his products, as well, and ten percent of your product. It's the cost of doing business and he has the business all in place. You don't. Count your blessings. Think of what you would have to do to get the trucks and the delivery people. Then they would have to get mapped out. You're getting a deal and Meyer gets to make a profit."

"That's what I like about you attorneys, you explain how we're getting screwed and then you try to make us like it while it's happening."

"Things could be worse. Try to see the good side."

Sure enough, as soon as we ended the call, things got worse.

"Mr. DiAngelo, the U.S. Attorney Smith on the phone."

"Good morning, Mr. Prosecutor."

"I guess that makes you Mr. Defense Attorney. Anyhow, do you happen to represent a couple of gentlemen, for lack of a better word, named Z and JB? Do any of your clients have names to go with these letters?"

"Why do you ask? I mean about my representation?"

"Because they are going to need attorneys, Mr. Mirage has agreed to talk. The first things that he talked about were them and the judge was tied in after he heard some of the tapes. We intend to issue a subpoena as soon as possible to be sure that they don't get any ideas to run."

"They won't run. They think it's still the old days."

"Will you be coming to the aid of Mr. Mirage?"

"I don't think so. He is no longer a defendant, he has immunity, he's not being prosecuted, and, if he is, the U.S. has Skip Livingston ready as a U.S. public defender and he couldn't get better for free anywhere. How could he afford to pay now anyway? You guys going to subsidize defense attorneys?"

"I'm just a poor public servant. Doing my job and offering you a chance to have your guys come in when we want them."

"No perp walk in front of the cameras?"

"Not anymore. The new boss doesn't need the press. He sees his job and gets it done."

"I'll tell them. Thanks for the heads up."

More bad news. It could wait.

CHAPTER
TWENTY-FOUR

"Would you gentlemen please agree to do away with opening arguments and proceed to presenting the evidence?"

Pukalski was the moving party and he went first. Attorney Tunney would be cross-examining. The testimony went smoothly enough showing the highest and best use of the property and, if not utilized, that it should be sold and the proceeds divided on a sixty/forty basis with Attorney Pukalski's client getting the higher percentage.

Attorney Tunney cross-examined as to the opinion of the expert presented. He was his usual smarmy self and didn't do much damage to the expert. The witness for the intended disposition of the property at the demise of the deceased parent made sure to outline the dictates of the last will and testament and how the intention should be clear. If it were clear and that simple, there would be no reason to have this hearing conducted.

We took a break for lunch and to give the court reporter a chance to rest. I called out for my messages. Billy and Zartan had called. I called back and they wanted to have a meeting. I insisted that this time we meet in my office. I was getting a little tired of cocktail meetings. This way I could be ready to move on to my other cases to make sure they didn't fall between the cracks or get backed up. It looked like the partition hearing would drag on for more than the day and a half we had hoped.

Back to the hearing, Tunney tried to outshout his opponent in the arguments over who was to be the recipient of the benefits of the property. Attorney Pukalski was no slouch in making his point either. I got them under control and the rest of the afternoon proceedings went as well as could be expected. We broke at four o'clock. I looked over several messages and ignored them.

I called Lola. Hearing her voice seemed like the tonic for what I needed.

"Obviously, the suspicions of your death have been greatly exaggerated."

"Mark Twain said 'rumors', I know that you knew that."

"Maybe I should have said, 'Unfortunately' the rumors of your death…"

"Ouch!"

"You should hurt so much."

"I may have made a mistake. Let's see, I'm calling to see if I can buy you dinner and I'm getting grief, am I missing something?"

"I should hope that you are missing me."

"I am. Terribly so."

"Is that why you never call? You know my birthday is this week and you haven't made plan one."

"Why do you think I am calling now?" (I actually didn't remember but Thank God, the Almighty inspired me to call.) "I was cleaning up my calendar so that you could make any demand you want for time and place."

"How about the rest of your life at your address?"

"I can stay there as long as you want."

"Not you, asshole, me with you."

"You know what, you caught me at a good, or weak, moment, we can talk about it."

"Talk is all I ever get. I can get that with my girlfriends, which is what I have scheduled for tonight. They didn't forget my birthday. We have plans for drinks after work."

"Good, I can save money on the cocktail hour and make it up on the present as well as the dinner."

"Why should I make time for you? You don't make time for me."

"I am making time as we speak." I took my best shot, "Well, they are taking you out before your birthday, so I am happy that you saved the real date for me."

"That's sweet of you, I knew you wouldn't forget. We were going to the Carlton for drinks. Do you want to meet me there or pick me up?"

"I need to see some people at Cioppino's. How about I pick you up? What time?"

"Six thirty should be enough time. We'll get there and gab at the bar with Domenic and they will have gag gifts for me to open. It is, however, the thought that counts with them. It's the gift that counts with you."

"I understand. See you at six thirty."

I punched in the phone numbers.

"Hello, L&S Jewelers."

"Pete?"

"Yes, is this Lou, our favorite attorney?"

"It sure is. Is Lenny there?"

"He's out to lunch. He should be back in a little bit. What do you need?"

"My head examined, but instead tell him to look for a nice round diamond. Not less than a carat, I guess. I think he knows her ring size. See what you can have ready for him when he comes back."

"Is this the move you want make, eh? God bless you."

"I'm counting on you, Pete. I know you will get the right stone for him. I'll be there in about an hour."

"We have to get the setting put together. I don't know if we can get it set that quickly. You know there are a lot of considerations that go into this. Oh, well, Lenny knows what you like and he'll do right by you. Make it two hours and you have a better shot."

"I'll be there."

I think I just went overboard. Impulse. Somehow, I must be vulnerable. Maybe that, or I am letting down my guard. Oh, well, you only live twice.

"Mr. D., a man says he's the Greek on the line."

"Thank you."

"Hello, Steve."

"Hey, Lou. Thanks, I know it's late but can I see you tonight?"

"Aw, Steve, I am in a jam. It's my lady's birthday. I'm in shit already as I didn't remember but I got a pass and I can't screw that up."

"You know, I agree with you. She's a nice lady and I don't want to get you in the middle of a mess. I do need to see you though, and it's important for both of us. What does tomorrow look like?"

"It looks like it's yours."

"Oh, great. I'll call you first thing and we'll arrange something."

"You got it."

I locked up and cleared the desk.

"See you ladies tomorrow." Headed out the parkway to L&S Jewelers. Parkway West outbound at five o'clock is a nightmare. Why anyone would live out that way is beyond me. Robinson Town Plaza is now a little city of itself. Lenny was in his diamond office when I arrived. He had some of his L.C. Greenwood collection on his desk as well as some estate stones. Pete was working on settings and got up to shake my hand and say hello.

"Luigi, how are you? Come on here, Pete's been working on some settings. I have some stones for you to look at."

Pete laughed with his head down. Lenny loves his work. He likes to show the diamonds that he buys. I found out by chance at a golf outing that he had the largest selection and collection of good diamonds anywhere. One after another he showed me the difference. He knew the one I liked the best right away but he showed me less expensive and more expensive ones, made me look through the magnifying eyepiece, all the while I'm thinking I have to get back to town through all that shit traffic. And he has to get it into the setting. Finally, "I know the one you want. Pete, can you put this in a platinum Italian solitaire setting? You know what, put the chip diamonds on each side. You taking the step again, is that it?"

"I don't know. I might. No matter, she deserves the ring."

"You're right. She's a nice lady. You're also a good guy, too. The Guy above must like you to find you such a nice lady. You are both good together. Smoke any good cigars lately?"

"I just got a shipment of Cubans last week. I wish I would have remembered, I would have brought you one."

Before too long, the ring was ready and gorgeous. I paid and was ready to go.

"The setting came from L.C. Greenwood's collection. Have you seen him lately?"

"We played golf a couple of weeks ago. I'll call him and get him out again soon. I think he had shoulder surgery. Listen, Lenny, I really have to run."

I made it out of the mall traffic and into three lanes of the Parkway West not moving toward the city. All the time, the ring is burning a hole in my pocket. A card! I have to get a card. There's a shop nearby or maybe even a gas station on the way. Oh, for God's sake. Why am I getting myself so worked up? It's only a birthday.

I made it to town and parked near the office and walked around the corner to Weldin's and picked out a card. Now back to the car and to the Carlton. I called Lola before I pulled away.

"How's it going?"

"Fine. We're having a decent time but the girls will have to start going to their other life such as cooking, second jobs, home duties and such. Where are you?"

"In front of my office."

"Ok. Why don't you pull up across the street from the entrance on Ross Street and I'll run over when you get here. I'll tell Kevin you said hello, goodbye."

"Thanks."

I drove uptown, parked across the street where there is no parking allowed and she hustled out the door, down the steps and over to the car.

"Nice to have a driver pick you up at the door."

"I'll tell Dean."

"Off to Cioppino's?"

"Unless you have had enough for one day."

"I've had enough wine. I could handle a little food."

Christian was by chance at the door when we arrived. He ushered us to the bar with warm welcomes. Lola excused herself and proceeded to the ladies room.

"Shit."

"What's the matter?"

"You wouldn't happen to have a small cake, would you? It's her birthday."

"Chocolate or white cake?"

"White."

"Coming up after dinner with 'Happy Birthday Lola' on it."

"Bless you."

"Mr. DiAngelo, nice to see you again."

"Thanks, Ashley."

"Macallan or Manhattan?"

"Macallan, thank you. Maybe a merlot for the lady. She's had a couple of wines already so I figure a lighter touch."

"No drink yet?"

"She just took my order. I ordered you a merlot. Can you handle another wine?"

"I only had the one at the Carlton. I was making sure that I could enjoy the wine and maybe more with you and I don't mean food."

"I can see I'm in for a night. Not sure if it's going to fun for me as I sense a little anger."

"No. It's not easy trying to keep my eye on the target with you. I'm never sure what will be the result of our relationship."

"Maybe I can ease your mind later."

The drinks arrived, she filled me in on the girl event, work efforts and such small talk. We finished at the bar and went back to the table where Greg came over and exchanged greetings before suggesting some items he was preparing. The suggestions were spectacular and the dinner went as well as anything could. We proceeded to the cigar bar in the other side of the restaurant. Nicole was a welcome hello from behind the bar, I had a Hennessy XO with a Galiano chaser and a decaf espresso.

"Shall I get you some vanilla ice cream as well?"

"Thanks, Nicole, maybe ask Christian to bring it. I think he may have something in mind."

Nicole gave me a quizzical look but proceeded to do as I asked.

She and Christian and Lisa, our waitress, then all proceeded to march into the bar while singing happy birthday. Talk about an event. Lola was taken completely by surprise, moved almost to tears, threw one arm around me and planted one on me. She was obviously moved beyond words. I then reached into my pocket and everybody was moved beyond words. Lisa and Nicole's jaws dropped as she opened the box. Three carats sitting in a square setting with another three or four carat cluster of smaller diamonds. She kissed me again with less passion and this time the wet part was coming from her eyes. I suspect her pantyhose were not dry anymore either. I started to think I may have gone over the top and later would really be a test as I had no chance to top this act by any physical performance. Of course, all the female staff clustered around in shifts to see the birthday present. It dawned on me that I hadn't said anything, not even happy birthday. Maybe I still had an escape exit somewhere. She was as happy as I had ever seen her and I was starting to ache for another brandy, a double I am sure. I had reacted to a situation and now felt like Laurel and Hardy, "What a fine mess you've gotten us into now".

After all the hoopla and the cake and ice cream, I now had to face the next chapter. I couldn't imagine that she was going to let me drive her home, or at least drive her home and leave immediately. It was as I suspected.

"Can we go to your house?"

"Were you expecting a bigger birthday present?"

"Maybe bigger and more beautiful, but not better. Oh, Lou, it's gorgeous. I do love you. You had such a wonderful evening planned for me and such a wonderful present, I feel like a creep for ever doubting you or thinking bad things about you."

Oh, boy. If she only knew. Oh, well, it's the thought that counts. I'll tell her after the evening is over.

We never made it past the downstairs bar. I think she ripped the buttons off my shirt and from her dress, as well, as she covered every inch of my body with kisses, especially the most important parts. I did practically nothing to enhance the situation. It was all her. I guess the birthday performance was above par and she felt she had to give payback.

After the usual climactic end, I was as wasted as she was. Birthday diamond sex is something special. Maybe I had better realize that the diamond means more than happy birthday. I looked over at her head on my chest. She was looking at the ring and twisting her hand this way and that… "Does this mean that I have to start looking for a dress soon?"

"I don't know what it means, but I do know this- that I love you, see, I said it, and I wanted you to be happy, and I wanted to give you a nice birthday present and this was it. Does it mean more? Probably after I think about it, it does. Is that enough for one day?"

"This is, I hope, the best birthday I have ever had. Let's go to bed. I think I might call off tomorrow. I might need you to drive me or lend me one of your cars to get fresh clothes."

"You still have some clothes in the spare bedroom."

"We can talk about all that tomorrow."

CHAPTER
TWENTY-FIVE

"Hello, Steve, what's the problem?"

"I'm on my way down to your office. I need to see you like I said last night."

"How soon will you be here?"

"In about twenty minutes."

"I won't be able to spend much time with you as I have a case we are finishing today. If you get here any longer than twenty minutes, I may not be able to see you at all."

"I'll be there."

I went over the notes from the testimony that we had heard so far. I outlined the factual scenario and whether it was starting to favor one side or the other. The list of witnesses only showed one remaining for the case in chief and one rebuttal. There could be others called as rebuttal depending on how the testimony went but it looked promising to get the case over by the end of the day.

"Mr. DiAngelo, Lola on the line."

"Good morning."

"It's a wonderful morning. I can hardly contain myself after last night. I still can't believe that I have this ring and almost a promise that I will have you. I had to call and say thank you for last night all around but especially how nicely you arranged everything and the ring is spectacular, almost as much as you are."

"Whoa, take it easy. It was just a last minute effort from a busy guy and it happened to click. What would I have done if you had refused the ring? Or the cake? Or the place?"

"I'm sure you would not have gotten the ring if you thought I would refuse. I couldn't make it any more clear what I have in mind. Making sure that you use that weapon only on me."

"Who has time for more than one woman? An old saying, if you hate a guy, wish a cummati on him. You have to satisfy two women and eventually the other one will want to take the place of the wife. If not permanently, then taking up more of your time. You have to be able to perform, be able to make up stories and on and on. It's too tough."

"Remember that for the future. By the way, what kind of gas does the Navigator use? It's almost on empty."

"Regular is fine. Listen, I have to go. I'll talk to you later."

I started to return to the case when the staff told me Steve was here.

"Send him in."

"Good morning, Counselor."

"Hi, Steve. What's so important?"

"I know you know about Mirage. I don't think you know about Billy and Zartan or the old man."

"What are you talking about?"

"I got a call from Billy. He wants me to meet with him. I got a call from Raphael as well. I am tied up with Raphael since way back but, since I'm Greek, I'm no family type guy. I'm like what they call freelance. I find out that they are both trying to get the same type setup from different interests. In other words, they are in competition. Billy is out of town and Raphael is local. In addition, there's Mirage. If he opens up, I'm not sure where I should be lined up. It gets worse. Two detectives have been following leads on that bartender that got killed. They are looking at some way out of town talent. Like from another country."

"Steve, do you have any idea how all this sounds? Why am I supposed to be hearing all this?"

"One- because you're my attorney and you represent all the other players as well. I need to know where I should go. I also need to know if you know where you should go. I need you so I can't afford to have you get hurt. I hear Mirage is opening up big time to get out of possible murder one charges as well as cocaine stuff. It's not going to be pretty."

"Your best bet is to avoid meeting with Billy and Zartan since you have no history with them. Stay as close to the old man as you can, but walk away from any conversations that deal with the whiskey business. Better yet, tell him that if he doesn't have anything pressing, you need some time to catch up with your lady and visit friends or family out of state. Try to get some distance for a while."

"What about the detectives? Have they talked to you?"

"No but they were asking around about me."

"Don't worry. They'll figure out that you had nothing to do with her murder."

"All right, sounds good. I hope you're right."

"It better be because I have to get to this hearing."

I tried to digest all that he had brought to me. This wasn't going to be a fun time in the old town tonight. I could see storm clouds on the horizon. Talk about two freight trains heading toward each other. And they both wanted to hire the man for whom I got the pardon and cleaned up his record so now he can be back in the bodyguard business. Hoping that is all that he does, I got back to work.

I went to the conference room and started the hearing. Fortunately, only one rebuttal witness and the record closed right after lunch. Now all I had to do was to review the testimony and make a determination some day in the near future.

I went to the mail that I hadn't opened for a few days and dictated responses to letters, reviewed status on a couple of divorces. It felt good getting the pile off my desk.

"Mr. DiAngelo, Tony on the phone."

"Good afternoon, Counselor."

"Hi, Tony."

"I hear you have a meeting tomorrow at your office."

"I have lots of meetings and some of them are even at my office."

"Do you think they would mind if I came?"

"Ask them."

"Can't you ask them?"

"No, I can't."

"Why not?"

"Because I am dealing with the people that requested the appointment. If they wanted you here, they would have asked you. If you want to come, you ask them."

"Easy, counselor, I'm just trying to make sure everybody is protected in their efforts to do business. You know the old man might call and ask you, but he figured you'd understand that I have a job to do as well."

"Even if he called, I can't do what you ask."

"Okay. I'll report back and maybe we might figure another way. Have a good day."

It looked like Steve was on to something. The players are starting to circle the wagons.

The rest of the afternoon went surprisingly without event.

Headed home at a regular hour and beat the traffic a little. It looked like it was going to be a gorgeous night. Maybe even espresso on the deck.

A quiet night's rest and the new day dawned.

I did all the morning routines and headed for the office. Usual traffic and slow downs. Parked and went to the office. After working on the testimony for a while, Jennifer announced that Billy and Zartan were here.

"Gentlemen."

"Good morning, Counselor."

"No Filo today?"

"No, he's out looking over some other properties."

"How can I help you today?"

"The hotel deal looks like it's a go. We were wondering about an export import license."

"Is this a coincidence?"

"What do you mean?"

"You both know what I mean. Other people have brought the same question to my office."

"Maybe it's a hot prospect. All of a sudden people want cars, do you think Chrysler and Ford can't go at it at the same time?"

"Chrysler and Ford only leave customers by the side of the road, not each other."

"We came to see if you can help us."

"I can help you, it's just that it's funny. What happens after I get you both the license is another story. But I suppose that is something for you guys to figure out."

We then hashed out all the motel agreement items and what they liked and didn't like, what might be negotiable and what I thought the seller would insist on having in the agreement. This was only opinion but we would explore in spite of what I thought the seller might want to do. We spent the better part of two hours on the agreement and then everybody was finished.

"Can we buy you lunch? I'm starved myself."

"I guess so."

"Where do you eat around here?"

"Usually Ruth's Chris."

"Yeah, let's go there. I could go for a steak."

"Let me wrap up the office."

"Okay, we'll go over and get a table."

I picked up the messages and Sherry handed me one. It was a call from Filo.

"He told me to tell you that it was important and not to interrupt you or announce that he had called so I held it here until your meeting broke up."

"Thank you."

I went back in and called.

"Counselor, good to hear from you. Can you talk?"

"They are waiting to buy me lunch across the square."

"Call me when you have time."

I headed out the door and noticed Detective Villalpando sitting behind the wheel of his car to the left of the office up the street.

"Good afternoon, Detective. Slumming or can't find a place to park uptown?"

"Actually waiting to see you. But I can wait until you have lunch with your friends."

"How do you know that?"

"They were in your office and went to Ruth's Chris. I didn't expect that they would not offer. If you had other plans you would be heading to your car so I made a guess."

"Good guess."

"Can I see you when you're done with lunch?"

"Sure, why not? Always willing to assist our finest working class."

"Thanks. I'll be sitting here waiting."

"Would you rather wait in our waiting room?"

"I might scare away your clients."

"Usually the locale gendarmes don't rattle them. The Feds get them nervous."

"I'll sit in the car. I might get an emergency call."

I went on my way to Ruth's Chris.

Kristin and Erin were at the bar getting drinks ready for the tables. Among them I saw my Manhattan. Erin followed me over to the table and set it down as Kristin greeted Billy and Zartan. Billy had a wine, Zartan opted for a coffee.

"So, you think this will go through or do you think they will dick around some more?"

"They will draw it out some more so as to have it appear that they have a position. They will then have it appear as though they are giving up something so to make you feel you are getting something that makes it more attractive to you. All the items that I said they will agree to change will almost all be agreeable. There are only one or two items that may really be items that they want to keep in the agreement."

"It's like a game with you guys."

"Not only us, it's the way people negotiate. Then there are some people who do not negotiate. Those are the people who don't care if the deal gets made or not. Those are the take it or leave it contracts. In this case, the other side wants to make the deal and have the property move off their hands. They have an incentive to deal. You have the same incentive. If they get obstinate, you will have to determine if you will give up anything. If you can't come to an agreement, then you will need to find another property, go through the same routine, pay me more money, figure out if the time lag is costing you any more than making this deal would cost by agreeing to any terms that you didn't like."

The lunch went on uneventfully as we bantered about Daily's and imports. They kidded with Kristin and some of the other staff inquiring if they would like to come work for them in the near future. Billy could turn on the charm when he wanted; Zartan was bereft of charm.

I was happy to allow them to pay the check and headed back to the office. Detective Villalpando was still in his car going through some papers. I knocked on the side window. He acknowledged me, put his papers in some sort of order and followed me into the office. I picked up my messages and put them on my desk as we sat down.

"What can I do for you today?"

"Did you ever hear of a Bison?"

"A what?"

"B I S O N, pronounced BEE ZAHN. It's a Russian bayonet style knife. It has a Bowie type blade, that is both sides are cutting edge. I ask because it makes a distinctive entry and exit wound. It was what was used on Allana. They aren't common in America but can be obtained online. They are the weapon of choice in Russia. The lab people had sent out for a report and this is what they produced. From your answer, I think I can assume that you have never heard of it."

"Good guess. This must be your day."

"We are now starting to wonder why this type of knife, why import export and a few other questions. Why Allana? She was pretty enough, but dangerous enough? I don't know."

"You don't think it was a lover's quarrel or that the ex-husband came back?"

"No. Not that we didn't make an investigation of him. You know we try to eliminate all the possibilities until we come up with the only possible solution. He had an alibi that stood up. We checked her security cameras at her apartment and there were no suspicious people coming or going, she didn't carry a lot of money and what she had on her was still in her purse so it wasn't robbery. She wasn't sexually assaulted so that was ruled out. It had to be something else. That's why I am here. I am trying to see if there was anything that you could think of that might help."

"Nothing that I could think of off the top."

"Did she say anything about who she was seeing or anything like that?"

"No. The only unusual… let me ask you, how much money did she have on her when you found her?"

"About forty dollars in mixed bills."

"She had over three thousand on her when she came to see me."

"Large denominations?"

"One hundred dollar bills."

"You deposited the money?"

"Right around the corner at PNC."

"That is interesting. Well, that might help give me some direction. Thanks for your time. Oh, and by the way, the real estate lady in New York was killed with the same type of knife."

He left and I looked at my messages. I put in a call to Leo.

"You called me, what's up?"

"It's the grand jury thing again. My wife's family is bustin' my balls and want to know what was going on in that New York property. Apparently some cops came over to see them. You know she has relatives that have relatives that sometimes do things that could lead to trouble. As soon as they saw her name I guess they thought there was some connection. Apparently there was something going on at the place. The people that were there doing something."

"It doesn't affect you at this point, does it?"

"Not as far as I can see. We didn't have any contact, only with the rental agent."

"Tell your relatives not to worry unless they actually went up to your place and used it."

"They say no."

"As long as they are telling the truth, they have nothing to worry about."

Next call to Tony.

"Counselor, thanks for calling back. Can we buy you dinner this weekend? Bring your friends, bring anybody you want, we need to see you."

"We need to see me?"

"Correct, we."

"Saturday looks open. Does that work for you?"

"It works. See you at the club around eight or eight thirty?"

"Figure about then. I'll try to make it at eight."

"Great, see you then."

Steve had cautioned me and now I am doing exactly the opposite of what he suggested. I just met with Billy and Zartan and now going to meet with the old man. Hey, nobody said I wasn't a gutsy guy or maybe just a hard-head.

CHAPTER TWENTY-SIX

"Hello, Gorgeous."

"Hey, yourself." She came over and kissed me gently but convincingly then she turned around.

"Would you mind fastening the clip through the knot? I can't seem to get it."

"Sure. You smell nice."

"I should. You bought it for me at Christmas. Ralph Lauren, Romance. Just what you had in mind, I suppose. Or have you forgotten?"

"Maybe it's old timers' disease."

"Thank you. Do I look okay?"

"I have yet to see you look bad. I'm not sure about the shoes. Red with a black dress? They're nice but I would probably have gone with black. Nice purse in any case."

"These weren't new and I was moving around the office a lot today and want to be sure that my feet don't bother me tonight. The purse was also a present from you."

"You'll get by with the shoes, don't worry. I bought the purse, too? Hmmm."

We proceeded to the car and Dean held the door for her to slide in. I climbed in after her.

"Where to, sir?"

"The club in New Kensington."

"Very good. Becoming a regular patron?"

"Make sure you forget that we ever went there in case you get a subpoena."

I had invited Chinky as well as Leo. I figured that I could get all my messages to everybody at once. We made really intimate small talk on the way. It never ceases to amaze me the change in a woman's behavior when they feel confident about the love that they want. They get almost cocky confident. I guess everybody gets that way when they succeed at something.

We were the first to arrive at the club. Tony was there to greet us and we proceeded to the bar for a drink. Shortly after, Leo and Carole and then Chinky and Marge arrived almost at the same time. We bantered for a bit and then were ushered to a table. The appetizers appeared without being ordered.

"May I suggest a red wine? We have a Pio Caesare 2000 that is drinking very well."

"Sure. Maybe you better have two bottles as there are six of us."

"I had that covered already."

Dinner went smoothly and we were to the coffee part of the dinner when Raphael appeared.

He went over to a distant table and Tony came over.

"Could you all excuse us for a minute? I need Lou over at the other table."

No objections were made, we moved over to the table. I also noticed some patrons started to enter the club as we traversed the room.

"Good evening, Counselor. Everything satisfactory for you?"

"Very good, thank you. You are very kind."

"I try to do right. Let me ask you, how is the license for Zartan and Billy going?"

"You'll have to ask them. I gave them the same answer when they asked about how your efforts were going. You all know that I can't and won't talk about clients to other people."

"I remember John Bazzano telling me that you were the only guy he knew that went to the grand jury and came back the same day."

"I also told them I wouldn't give any information about my client as the client wasn't committing or intending to commit a crime so I wouldn't provide what they wanted. That's the only reason that you invited me here tonight, is it?"

"No, it isn't. I want to talk to you and your friend from Daily's. I want to get an exclusive on the distribution of the product through their company. If we can access their contacts exclusively, then we won't care about anybody else."

"That's a business decision that they will have to make. I don't represent them."

"You can talk to your buddy and ask him to consider it. We can make it worth it to them."

"Do you want me bring him over and you can ask him?"

"Why don't you do that?"

Tony jumped in and spoke up that he would gather him over.

"Are we moving to this table one at a time?"

"No, just you, Mr. Predmore, and then we should be finished. I should like to get an agreement with your company that the product that we provide will be an exclusive in its category for distribution. We could make some financial arrangement that would be beneficial to your company's interests."

"I can't speak for my bosses, but I will see what they might want to do."

"That's all I can ask. You know that I know Tony and Meyer from way back. I hope they won't forget or think less of me because I happen to have had you available to ask through the counselor here."

"I'm sure that they won't."

The parley broke up and we went on with our evening.

Somehow, some way, instinct, or the accumulation of years of experience sets off a signal, you just feel that something is out of the ordinary. Guys call it a hunch. Women call it intuition. I had been warned. A problem might appear. A lot of action going on in the same direction. Makes you start to look over your shoulder.

We chatted the night away, had a few more drinks and called it a night. I couldn't say no to the request to have Lola spend the night. She had the ring, just as well that she had me. Felt a lot different. A completely different feeling now. The romancing was over and now she didn't have to be nice anymore if she didn't want to be nice. I felt a similar feel that we were an item that was finalized although it wasn't. There were a lot of things to be determined. This could be one of those long waiting periods as we hadn't discussed any thing permanent or any immediate plans.

Dean dropped us off with a cheery goodnight as he was off duty without a long ride yet to complete. We headed into the downstairs bar room through the garage.

Lola turned into me and put her arms around my neck.

"Have I told you that I love you since we got home?"

We barely made it to the couch. I never knew women could be so aggressive. Good thing it was an older suit as she fairly destroyed the zipper and I could only get one shoe off before she started looking for ways to make me scream for joy. We continued for the better part of an hour as she released me to try to take my turn at pleasing her. Thank God for multiple orgasms for women. Eventually she felt that she had enough and wanted to be sure that I didn't go to bed incomplete. She didn't let me or herself down.

I almost had a heart attack then when she said, "I'll make the coffee in the morning. I want to get used to being here."

CHAPTER TWENTY-SEVEN

I never heard her get up. Unusual, as I hear everything while I am in bed. I could smell the coffee.

She appeared in the doorway, peeking in and I waved at her.

"I didn't want to disturb you, but what would you like for breakfast?"

"Coffee, anisette toast, sausage. I'll skip the eggs and cereal today."

"You're easy. I was ready to make you want to never have me leave."

"I wish you would go slow on that. You realize I still have to get it in my mind that any kind of a step has been taken. Best for you to go slow."

"I'll go as slow as you want but I still want to show you that it's better with me than without me. As if you didn't know that already."

"Look at it the other way. I wouldn't want to find out how it is without you. So don't screw up."

"Coffee is ready and the rest will be also when you make it downstairs."

I rolled out of bed, got a robe and made it to the kitchen.

"I made a pot of traditional blend, whatever that is. It was the lowest one on the shelf and looked as though you drank it before."

"That will be fine."

Breakfast went well. We shared the Sunday paper, which she had retrieved from the driveway. Then we started to get ready to go pay our respects to the Almighty. Father Jim from Lower Burrell and Father Tom would be doing double duty today as the Monsignor was visiting around the Diocese. Fund-raisers, celebration of anniversaries of ordinations, new deacons, there would no end to the reason to get together. Father Ken was up from Florida. It was a full house. We bantered with them all. Father Ken noticed the ring and went for the jugular.

"You're finally going to get rid of having that confessional problem."

I suddenly had a weak feeling in my legs. "It was merely a birthday present, Padre. Don't get stars in her eyes."

"Have I said anything except 'Thank you' for the ring? I don't have to say anything, I just show the ring and let everyone jump to conclusions. Eventually it will become real. I learned patience when you're holding four aces in a poker game."

"Well said, Lola. Don't let him bluff you."

"Don't you have something to do, like go inside and say Mass for all the happy people in the church?"

"Just keep your hands out of the collection basket, you don't get a contingent fee for passing the basket."

The religious proceedings went smoothly and we left for the car after the final goodbyes. We went back home and did some household chores, pulled dinner out of the freezer, made some popcorn and watched the Steelers take a loss to Baltimore. Dinner and no trouble. To bed and up for the week's adventures. I don't know if I will get used to sleeping all night with someone beside me. It happened once before so I will probably be able to get used to it again.

"Good morning, all."

The staff was up and at it when I walked into the office.

I started in on some of the case files that needed attention. Halfway through the morning, the intercom interrupted me.

"Mr. D, two detectives in the waiting room."

"Tell them I will be with them shortly."

It took me about ten minutes to get to a logical stopping point. I went to the waiting room.

"Gentlemen, good morning."

"Hello, Attorney."

"Both of you this time?"

"Can we have a few minutes?"

"Come on in. Coffee or Water?"

"You know what, I could use a cup of coffee. Would you mind?"

"Jennifer, get a cup of coffee for the gentleman. Tell her how you like it."

We proceeded to my office.

"You know Mirage has been talking?"

"I didn't but I have advised him as to what his options are and what I think he can expect."

"The government attorneys don't usually let us in on anything that they are doing. They think that they are the only people that can be trusted, but in this case there is a homicide where the state has the only jurisdiction so they have provided to our supervisor some limited inside information. We found out that the real estate agent in New York, which we agreed with the Feds may make it a federal offense, was related to the bartender from Bob's Garage. They were also killed with the same type of knife. We also found out that Mirage told them the bartender had been dating a large, not overweight, but big guy. A blonde guy with a funny accent. Not American, we think. What does that do for you?"

"Makes me all tingly inside that you are going to tell me you have the killer, right?"

"Not have the killer, but might have some suspects. You have a client Leo Parks, right?"

"That's right."

"He is married to a related girl, right?"

"That's right."

"They have a place in upstate New York as well, right?"

"What is this? One step at a time. Are you going to tell me something or do I have to wait until final Jeopardy?"

"Okay, it appears that some of the friends of the family members were using the place in New York. There was a stopover for some young girls and some other items were being transferred. They were thinking of starting a meth lab, but then there was a heist. Did you hear about the almost eight hundred cases of vodka that were stolen. This was the collector's edition with gold-plated bands around the bottle."

"Worth about two million if I recall correctly, from an airport holding area and no clues?"

"That's the one, Counselor."

"I do remember reading about it."

"Now the problem is dumping the goods. First it had to be stored somewhere. Airport in New York robbed. Keep the booty in New York."

"The upstate house?"

"Hey, you catch on. Real estate agent walks in and finds out more than she should. She gets whacked. Bartender in Pittsburgh gets close to a certain guy with a funny accent, pow. Now, all we need to find out is who the guy is. We have the motive, we have the suspect, now we need the guy. Mirage couldn't help the Feds or us as he never got to meet the guy. But we think your clients have met him or them. We think they are dealing with whoever did the real estate agent and the bartender. What can you tell us?"

"I wish this were like the movies and everybody else had the answers and the cops were dumb flatfoots, but, congratulations, you guys are dazzling me as I know none of this."

"We have access to public filings and license. We know that you are representing several groups applying for import export licenses and a hotel license. Doesn't that seem coincidental?"

"I don't get paid to make those kinds of guesses. My job is to perform what I get retained to do so as long as it's not illegal."

"We know that you don't do anything illegal, Counselor, but if you can prevent the commission of a crime, I would think you would take action."

"I don't see any crime on the horizon. I have no facts or knowledge that any crime has been committed by anybody I represent and certainly have no idea that they are going to commit any sort of crime."

"Okay. What about Daily Juice?"

"What about them?"

"You know that they might be distributing product on a lease agreement."

"They have trucks and they have people that deliver product. What's wrong with that?"

"Seems like it all ties in nicely."

"It's all legal."

We bantered about for a bit more and then they decided that I couldn't be of any real help so it ended. I was at the same place that I was when they arrived. A lot of info that I already knew and nothing new that was of any help in what I was trying to do, represent my clients.

The rest of the day went fairly smoothly. I then got a call from the Greek.

"Counselor, this is a warning, be careful of any meetings that you get asked to attend for the next couple of days."

"What does that mean?"

"It means be careful. Be on your toes. That's all." and he hung up the phone.

I got back into the office files and Tony called.

"Counselor, I hear you did real good and the delivery and the licenses are going through. Can we meet at the hotel in Tarentum some time soon? I need to finalize a couple of things."

"Not at the club?"

"No, I don't want to be out that far or that late, how's your schedule?"

"How about tomorrow?"

"Around eight o'clock?"

"I think I can make that."

"Good, see you tomorrow."

And the Greek said to be careful of any meetings. Sometimes I wonder how word spreads so fast. I finished up the decision on the Partition case and called it a day. I was lost in thought on the way home and didn't notice the car behind me until he turned on to my street as he had turned on the street before. Then I saw it was Filo. He pulled alongside.

"You've had a big day, Counselor. Where's the meeting?"

"Oh sweet Jesus! How do you know about that?"

"It's how you stay alive, by knowing things. Where?"

"That motel in Tarentum across the bridge in the shopping mall."

"What time?"

"Eight o'clock."

"Don't get there until eight thirty. Trust me. Do not get there before eight thirty."

He then drove off.

I needed a Macallan as badly as I had ever needed one. Too many people know about this meeting and now I have been warned and basically called off from going. I was ashamed of myself as I was looking around the garage and the downstairs room. I did it with the Walther PPK from the car. I was then happy that the only thing around was a dead mouse in a sticky trap.

Macallan never tasted so good. I was tempted to finish more than I should but decided to have some spaghetti and a salad followed by a cigar with espresso and a Strega to make all my anxieties disappear. I had the espresso out on the deck and watched the birds, squirrels and chipmunks run around. Sleep would be welcome tonight if my mind would be able to stop racing and wondering about tomorrow.

CHAPTER TWENTY-EIGHT

The day went fairly smoothly. I got the paperwork done on the transfers, got the Partition file off my desk, had a pre-trial conciliation in the morning.

"Mr. DiAngelo, Lola on the line."

"Good morning."

"How good? I haven't heard from you and started to wonder. Can I buy you lunch today?"

"You know what, I have another conciliation after lunch. I could meet you at the Carlton in about twenty minutes."

"See you at table ten in twenty minutes."

I got the files together and started for the door. The phone buzzed.

"Mr. D, it is JZ."

Ok, I'll take it."

"Hello, Luigi, coma esta?"

"I couldn't be better, but I was on my way out the door so I can't be on this call too long."

"I won't keep you. I just wanted to be sure all the apps were in order and we are good to go." "They are all done. I made that known last week. Didn't you get the word?"

"Sometimes people don't talk about things that they should share. Thank you, Counselor."

I began again to lunch. Thought that the call was strange but not my problem.

Janet was her usual happy self and greeted me as usual.

"You must be moving up in the world, your lady called to make the reservation."

"You know I'm glad she did because I didn't think of it. At 11:30 I can usually get a good table. Unless someone comes or reserves it early like John Weinstein of Michael Lamb."

"Don't worry, they would be more than happy to move."

I felt her arm inside mine and she kissed me gently on the cheek, "How's my big and handsome Romeo?"

"Sounds like a line from a song."

"It is. I think it follows 'how I won you, I will never, never know.'"

"May I seat you two before you make everyone else in the place nauseated?"

David waited on us and provided her wine and my Manhattan as though the drinks were waiting for us to arrive.

"So, how have you been and how is your week going, or shouldn't I ask?"

"Day is going fine. I have a meeting tonight. Wrapping up some transfers and corporate matters. I had an odd call this morning about one of the applications, just struck me odd."

"I'm sure you'll work it out. When are we getting together?"

"What do you call this?"

"Lunch."

"I'll work you into my schedule. Give me a day to arrange my life."

We finished lunch, she left and paid the check. I wondered how many lunches the diamonds were worth and whether I would ever catch up. Oh well, everything doesn't always even out.

The rest of the day went okay. I made my way to the car and then started the drive out Route 28 to the Tarentum Bridge. As usual, the traffic was a nightmare. Finally, past Harmarville, it opened up a bit. Getting across the bridge and into the parking lot, I was thirty minutes later that I was told to be there and on time as I was warned to be there. I thought I saw the two guys that I met at the Howard Johnson's parking lot in Monroeville, Jojo and Chuckie Z. They weren't clearly visible as I parked the car and maybe the parking lot triggered a false memory.

I was about to get out of the car when a shadow covered the side window and I looked up to see the Greek.

"Good evening, Counselor. Don't get out of the car. I'll pull around and you follow me."

I waited as he suggested. I could tell by his voice that there were no options. He pulled around and I followed him out of the lot and down toward New Kensington and the club. As we were pulling out of the lot, I did see the two guys from the parking lot and also a tall blonde man in front of them with Tony beside the tall blonde man.

We proceeded past the club to a large estate-type house with large ground and a palatial house in the middle. Steve pulled up, parked and led me in to the garage and down a flight of steps to a room that was eerie in how quiet it seemed to be. If it were soundproof, I would not have been surprised.

"Have a seat, Lou. Something to drink?"

"If you have Macallan, I would like one neat."

"Please excuse the 18 as the 25 is too expensive and too hard to get."

"That'll be fine."

Raphael and Sam's daughter came silently into the room. They had serious looks on their faces. She looked almost shaken.

"Thank you for coming and thank you for following the instructions from the Greek. You did the right thing with the applications. You did the right thing on behalf of both of the competing interests. What you didn't know was that there was a third interest. The vodka thief, the meth lab, the real estate broker and the bartender were all part of a move that wasn't kosher. The local police have just made an arrest of a foreign national. He will be sent to New York to the Federal people. I think that Tony may have tried to escape and was shot and killed by the police. Your friend Leo may not be involved but he didn't tell you everything. Car salesmen can ship cars. They can also ship contents and equipment for the cars in separate containers. Tony wanted to get too big. He got involved with the Russian. They wanted to do meth. The place in New York was perfect. The realtor came out without letting them know. She walked in on an ongoing lab. She had to go. The bartender was fooling around with the Russian. She heard too much of a conversation between Tony and him. She tried to squeeze Tony, so Tony told the Russian. Two for two. Now all was clear for the move. Problem was getting the license in Tony's name. Next best is sitting here beside me. Good as gold… if anything happened to her, Tony still couldn't get the license in his name. Her father, Sam, could. That was where the line was crossed. I didn't care about the realtor or the bartender. That was a shame but not my concern. Sam was my concern. We weren't sure who or why. Fortunately, we have a few people in the offices that arrest and prosecute. Mirage was supposed to get in jail, get the information and maybe bump the contact. Fortunately for us, he also knew who fingered the move on Sam. Tony. So, now Sam's daughter has the license, the import export is ready to go, the good guys- us- are winning this round. And you know what? We ain't doing anything illegal. If I would have known how easy it is to make money legit we would have done this years ago. You got Steve the permit to carry. I think he was on loan to the police. My guys from the parking lot have been making sure that you didn't get hurt and I made sure that you got paid. Your friend Chinky was able to get distribution for us, as well. Billy and Zartan and those guys are happy to have a motel. Maybe you get a honeymoon suite when you take the leap. What so you think about that, Counselor?"

"I think that I am glad that I accepted the drink offer."

"You're a good lad. Not everybody you work for is such a good guy, however. Is there anything else I can do for you?"

My head was swimming. I was sure that Tony was dead already and probably no one would get prosecuted. I was also sure that the two other guys had the Russian in the hands of federal handlers. Sam was probably smiling down on us.

"I can't think of anything. I probably could use a good night's sleep after all the action that went on around me tonight."

"Are our accounts square money-wise?"

"I think so."

"Good night then."

Steve motioned me to follow him again."

"You did good following instructions, Counselor. I think you may have been in the middle or at least in the way if you had arrived on time. It ain't like Court, sometimes late is good."

I got into the car and headed for home. My cell phone rang.

"Lola, what's up?"

"How's your schedule looking?"

I thought of the late Tony, the late Sam, the soon to be late Russian, being late for the meeting. "Sure, come on over. We can do the late, late, late show tonight."

WA

www.ingramcontent.com/pod-product-compliance
Lightning Source LLC
Chambersburg PA
CBHW060543200326
41521CB00007B/460

9 7 8 1 6 3 3 8 5 1 1 8 4